Southern Living

SLOW-COOKER
COOKBOOK

Beef Brisket with Fall
Vegetables, page 99

Southern Living®

SLOW-COOKER
COOKBOOK

Compiled and Edited by
Jane E. Gentry

Oxmoor
House®

ISBN-13: 978-0-8487-3150-2
ISBN-10: 0-8487-3150-6
Library of Congress Control Number: 2005937452
Printed in the United States of America
Second Printing 2009

Oxmoor House, Inc.
Editor in Chief: Nancy Fitzpatrick Wyatt
Executive Editor: Susan Carlisle Payne
Art Director: Keith McPherson
Managing Editor: Allison Long Lowery

Southern Living®
Slow-Cooker Cookbook

Editor: Jane Elizabeth Lorberau
Nutrition Editor: Anne Cain, M.S., R.D.
Digital Production Editor: Julie Boston
Senior Designer: Melissa Jones Clark
Copy Chief: L. Amanda Owens
Photography Director: Jim Bathie
Senior Photo Stylist: Kay E. Clarke
Associate Photo Stylist: Katherine Eckert
Director, Test Kitchens: Elizabeth Tyler Austin
Assistant Director, Test Kitchens: Julie Christopher
Test Kitchens Professionals: Kathleen Royal Phillips,
Catherine Crowell Steele, Ashley T. Strickland
Director of Production: Laura Lockhart
Senior Production Manager: Greg A. Amason
Production Manager: Terri Beste-Farley
Production Assistant: Faye Porter Bonner

Contributors
Designer: Nancy Johnson
Photographers: Mark Gooch, Lee Harrelson
Indexer: Mary Ann Laurens
Interns: Meg Kozinsky, Rachel Quinlivan, Mary Catherine Shamblin

Cover: Thai-Style Ribs, page 116
Back Cover: Mocha Pudding Cake, page 174; Mu Shu Chicken Wraps, page 133;
Spicy Black-and-Red Bean Soup, page 216; Kelley's Famous Meat Loaf, page 107

To order additional publications, call 1-800-765-6400.

For more books to enrich your life, visit **oxmoorhouse.com**
To search, savor, and share thousands of recipes, visit **myrecipes.com**

contents

slow-cooker success

It's easy to become a slow-cooker professional—just follow these simple and handy tips and secrets.

Slow-Cooker Options

• Slow cookers come in round and oval shapes, as well as in a variety of sizes—from 16 ounces to 7 quarts, with half sizes in between.

• Some new slow cookers cook at a slightly hotter temperature than older models. If using a newer model, check for doneness at the lower end of the time range. If your cooker seems to boil contents, you may want to check for doneness a little early.

• Cookers with removable inserts are easier to clean than one-piece units.

• A new product on the market is an external timer device that allows you to set your cooking time; when that time has expired, the timer automatically switches the cooker to warm. Simply plug the timer into the wall outlet, and then plug your cooker into the timer.

VersaWare ▶
You'll love what you can do with this extreme temperature stoneware. You have the option of preparing your slow-cooker recipes the traditional way by placing the stoneware on the base, or you can use the stoneware for baking dishes in the oven. You can even brown meat directly in the stoneware!

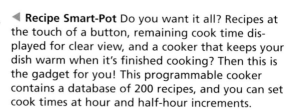

Smart-Pot ▶
Available in 5- and 6-quart sizes, this slow cooker is programmable to cook either 4 to 6 hours on HIGH or 8 to 10 hours on LOW. The crowning jewel of this appliance is that the cooker automatically switches to warm when the cooking time is done. An added benefit is that the insert is dishwasher safe.

◀ Recipe Smart-Pot Do you want it all? Recipes at the touch of a button, remaining cook time displayed for clear view, and a cooker that keeps your dish warm when it's finished cooking? Then this is the gadget for you! This programmable cooker contains a database of 200 recipes, and you can set cook times at hour and half-hour increments.

Tips & Techniques

- Removing the cooker lid during cooking releases a great deal of heat, so resist the urge to lift the lid and peek. Each time you remove it when not required, you'll need to increase the cooking time by 20 to 30 minutes.
- There's no need to stir ingredients unless a recipe specifically calls for it. Always layer ingredients as the recipe directs.
- Remember that 1 hour on HIGH equals approximately 2 hours on LOW. A bonus to cooking on LOW is that recipes can generally cook a little longer than the recipe states without becoming overdone.
- Trim excess fat from meats. If desired, brown meat in a skillet or a broiler to remove fat and then drain the fat before adding the meat to the cooker.
- When making roasts or stews, pour liquids over meats and use only the liquids specified in the recipes. While amounts may sometimes seem low, more juices cook out of the ingredients and there's less evaporation than in traditional cooking methods.
- Cuts of meat with high fat content can be cooked without added liquid when the cooker is set on LOW. According to personal preference, add a little liquid to produce a delicious gravy.
- You can thicken juices and make gravy by removing the lid and cooking on HIGH for the last 20 to 30 minutes.

Entertaining Secret

Serve hot drinks or appetizers in your slow cooker at your next party. Be sure to use the LOW setting.

Test Kitchen Staff Tidbits

Corned Beef and Cabbage (page 101) has been a personal favorite since I was a little girl, so I developed a version for the slow cooker that is fork-tender and full of flavor.
—Elizabeth Austin
Test Kitchen Director

Chunky Minestrone (page 219) in the slow cooker takes me back to childhood. When the aroma welcomes me from a long day of work or gardening, it's like coming home to my mom's kitchen.
—Julie Christopher
Assistant Test Kitchen Director

As a working mother of growing twin boys, I am always on the run. Developing recipes like Squash and Cornbread Casserole (page 236) ensures that I get a head start on dinner.
—Elise Weis, Test Kitchen Staff

I like to use my slow cooker to make Roasted Chicken with Vegetables (page 130). I bone and chop the meat to use in recipes that call for chopped cooked chicken.
—Kathleen Phillips
Test Kitchen Staff

Food Facts

- **Dried beans** take longer to tenderize if combined with sugar and acid before softening. To achieve the desired tenderness, soak beans before adding them to the cooker and add sugar and acid only after beans have cooked until tender.
- **Dairy and seafood** tend to break down when cooked for extended periods. Unless otherwise instructed, add milk, cream, and sour cream during the last 15 minutes of cooking; add seafood within the last hour.
- Vegetables often cook slower than meats and, therefore, need direct contact with the bottom and sides of the cooker. Place **vegetables under meats** in the slow cooker unless otherwise instructed.

- The more fat, or "marbling," a cut of **meat** has, the more liquid it releases during cooking, requiring less liquid to be added.
- For **roasts and poultry** larger than 2 to 3 pounds, cut in half—these smaller portions ensure thorough cooking.
- **Meats** cooked in a slow cooker don't brown as they do in the oven or a skillet. To add visual appeal and extra flavor, you can brown meat in a bit of oil in a skillet before adding to the cooker.

- **Fresh herbs and spices** are better than dried for extended slow-cooking times— they take longer to release their flavors.
- When using **dried herbs,** we recommend whole to crushed or ground.
- **Pasta** retains the best texture when cooked separately according to package directions and then added to the slow cooker during the last 30 minutes of cooking.
- Cooking **rice** can be tricky in a slow cooker. For the best results, always use long-grain converted rice.

Slow-Cooker Safety

- When cooking raw meats and poultry, the U.S. Department of Agriculture recommends using HIGH heat for the first hour to make sure ingredients reach a safe temperature quickly. Then you can reduce the heat to LOW for the remainder of cooking.
- You can omit the HIGH heat for the first hour in recipes that brown the meat first, since precooking jump-starts the initial temperature of ingredients.
- Defrost any frozen foods before cooking to make sure the contents of the crock reach a safe temperature quickly.

- Always fill a slow cooker at least half-way full and no more than two-thirds full in order for food to reach a safe temperature.
- Use the specified slow-cooker size to ensure proper levels of food, thorough cooking, and safe temperatures. If you use a different size, cooking time may vary accordingly.

Easy Cleanup

- Always allow the slow cooker insert to cool completely before washing it. Cold water poured over a hot insert can cause cracking.
- Never immerse a slow cooker in water. Simply unplug it, and wipe clean with a cloth.
- A new product that simplifies slow-cooker cleanup is a clear, heavy-duty plastic liner made to fit 3- to 6½-quart oval and round slow cookers. It's as simple as fitting the plastic liner inside your slow cooker before adding the recipe ingredients. When you're finished cooking, simply serve the meal directly from the cooker. Once the cooker has cooled, just toss the plastic liner along with the mess.

Test Kitchen Staff Tidbits

My meat loaf is finally famous (page 107)! While my original version bakes in the oven, I'm thrilled to know that it can be made in the slow cooker and turn out just as delicious.
—Kelley Wilton, Test Kitchen Staff

Holidays are about family and friends, and I believe time should be spent in fellowship with those you love, not in the kitchen. So I devel-oped recipes with the busy holidays in mind.

After a long day of shopping and wrapping gifts, prop your feet up and enjoy a steaming bowl of my Grandma Dean's Chicken and Dressing (page 231)!
—Kristi Carter, Test Kitchen Staff

The funny thing about this book is that a lot of the recipes I developed are Southern dishes—and I'm from Minnesota! It was a proud moment knowing I finally crossed the regional boundary.
—Nicole Faber, Test Kitchen Staff

menus

Put a meal together in no time
with these slow cooker–inspired menus.

Southern Veggie Delight

serves 8

Mexican Corn Pudding   *Sweet and Hot Black-Eyed Peas*

Nana's Collard Greens

Comfort Food

Mexican Corn Pudding

2   large eggs
1   (15.25-ounce) can whole kernel corn,
      undrained
1   (14¾-ounce) can cream-style corn
1   (4.5-ounce) can diced green chiles
1   (8½-ounce) box corn muffin mix (we
      tested with Jiffy)
½   cup butter, melted
1   teaspoon cumin

● Whisk eggs in a large bowl. Add remaining ingredients, and mix well. Pour into a lightly greased 3-quart oval slow cooker.
● Cover and cook on LOW 5 hours or until edges are set. Let stand 5 minutes. Stir before serving. Makes 8 servings.

Slow-Cooker Size: 3-quart oval

Prep: 21 minutes
Cook: 5 hours
Other: 5 minutes

Extra-Special

Give this pudding added "yum" by adding ¼ cup cheese of your choice at the end of the cooking time. Recover the crock for 10 minutes or until the cheese is melted; then serve.

Simple ingredients **dress up** a box of corn muffin mix.

Sweet and Hot Black-Eyed Peas

1   (16-ounce) package dried black-eyed
        peas
¼   cup butter
2   cups hot water
2   cups chopped onion
1½ cups chopped red bell pepper
2   cups chopped green bell pepper
1   small jalapeño pepper, seeded and
        chopped
2   garlic cloves, minced
1   teaspoon salt
½   teaspoon ground red pepper
¼   teaspoon black pepper

• Sort and wash peas; place in a 5-quart slow cooker.
Cover with water 2 inches above peas; let soak 8 hours.
Drain. Return peas to slow cooker.
• Combine butter and remaining ingredients in slow
cooker. Cover and cook on HIGH 4 hours. Makes 9 servings.

Slow-Cooker Size: 5-quart

Prep: 18 minutes
Cook: 4 hours
Other: 8 hours

Soak Up the Flavor

Dried beans and peas are
ideal for slow cooking
because they really soak
up ingredient flavors when
they're cooked over long
periods of time.

Nana's Collard Greens

4   bacon slices
1   large carrot, chopped
1   large onion, chopped
2   garlic cloves, minced
2   to 3 tablespoons balsamic vinegar
4   (1-pound) packages fresh collard greens,
        washed, trimmed, and chopped
1½ cups low-sodium fat-free chicken broth
½   teaspoon dried crushed red pepper
½   teaspoon salt
¼   teaspoon black pepper

Prep: 20 minutes
Cook: 1 hour, 15 minutes

Make-Ahead Tip

You can make these greens up to 2 days ahead and reheat just before serving, if desired.

● Cook bacon slices in a Dutch oven until crisp. Remove bacon, and drain on paper towels, reserving 2 tablespoons drippings. Crumble bacon.
● Cook carrot in hot bacon drippings in Dutch oven over medium-high heat, stirring occasionally, 5 minutes. Add onion, and cook, stirring occasionally, 5 minutes or until carrot and onion begin to caramelize. Add garlic; cook, stirring constantly, 30 seconds. Add balsamic vinegar, and cook 30 seconds. Add collards, crumbled bacon, broth, and remaining ingredients.
● Bring to a boil; cover, reduce heat, and simmer 1 hour or until collards are tender. Makes 6 to 8 servings.

Add a sprinkling of
pepper sauce to
each serving for extra kick.

Kids' Night

serves up to 12

Spicy Vegetable-Beef Soup   *grilled cheese sandwiches*

ice cream sundaes

▬▬ ▬ ▬ ▬ ▬ ▬ ▬▬ ▬ ▬ ▬ ▬ ▬ ▬▬

15 Minutes or Less to Prep

Spicy Vegetable-Beef Soup

1   pound ground chuck
1   onion, chopped
2   (28-ounce) jars tomatoes, peppers, and
       spices pasta sauce (we used Newman's
       Own Sockaroni)
1   (10½-ounce) can condensed beef broth,
       undiluted
1½ cups water
½   cup dry red wine
1   (14½-ounce) can garlic and olive oil
       petite diced tomatoes, undrained
1   (10-ounce) can diced tomatoes and
       green chiles, undrained
1   (16-ounce) package frozen mixed
       vegetables, thawed
½   teaspoon pepper

● Cook beef and onion in a large skillet 7 minutes, stirring until beef crumbles and is no longer pink; drain well.
● Combine beef mixture, pasta sauce, and remaining 7 ingredients in a 5-quart slow cooker.
● Cover and cook on HIGH 6 hours or on LOW 12 hours. Makes 4 quarts.

Slow-Cooker Size: 5-quart

Prep: 12 minutes
Cook: 6 hours or 12 hours

Spicy!

If you don't want the spice, substitute your favorite flavor of diced tomatoes for the tomatoes with green chiles.

Eye-Opening Comfort

serves 8

Caramel Apple Oatmeal   *Black Pepper-Brown Sugar Bacon*

Sparkling Apple Juice

▬▬ ▬ ▬ ▬ ▬▬ ▬ ▬ ▬ ▬ ▬ ▬ ▬ ▬ ▬ ▬ ▬ ▬ ▬

Caramel Apple Oatmeal

3	cups uncooked regular oats
1	cup chopped dried apples
¾	cup firmly packed light brown sugar
1	vanilla bean, split
2	teaspoons ground cinnamon
¼	teaspoon salt
4	cups milk
3	cups apple cider
3	tablespoons butter, divided
1	cup raisins

• Combine first 8 ingredients and 2 tablespoons butter in a 3½-quart slow cooker.
• Cover and cook on LOW 3 to 4 hours or until thickened.
• Remove vanilla bean; scrape seeds from inside of bean, discarding bean. Stir vanilla seeds, remaining 1 tablespoon butter, and raisins into oatmeal. Serve warm. Makes 8 servings.

Slow-Cooker Size: 3½-quart

Prep: 6 minutes
Cook: 4 hours

Make-Ahead Tip

This oatmeal reheats well in the microwave if you want to prepare it the night before. It also keeps up to 3 days in the fridge.

Chock-full of apple and raisins, a bowl of **creamy caramel-flavored goodness** starts the day off right.

Black Pepper-Brown Sugar Bacon

12 ounces thick bacon slices
3   tablespoons cracked black pepper
1   cup firmly packed dark brown sugar

● Quarter each slice of bacon, and arrange in a single layer in an aluminum foil-lined broiler pan. Press cracked black pepper onto bacon slices; cover evenly with brown sugar.
● Bake at 425° for 25 minutes or until done. Let stand 2 to 3 minutes or until sugar is set. Makes 12 servings.

Prep: 5 minutes
Cook: 25 minutes
Other: 3 minutes

Test Kitchen Secret

To easily apply the brown sugar, use a teaspoon to sprinkle sugar over the bacon strips; then press the sugar into the bacon with your fingers.

Sparkling Apple Juice

4   cups apple juice, chilled
4   cups ginger ale, chilled

● Combine apple juice and ginger ale. Serve over ice. Makes 8 cups.

Prep: 2 minutes

Sunday Crock Supper

serves 6

Roast with Onion-and-Mushroom Gravy

Simple Mashed Potatoes   steamed sugar snap peas

bakery rolls   iced tea

Roast with Onion-and-Mushroom Gravy

Due to the salty nature of the soup mix, use low-sodium broth for this roast.

1	(2.5-pound) boneless beef chuck shoulder roast, trimmed
¾	teaspoon pepper
1	(14-ounce) can low-sodium beef broth
1	(10¾-ounce) can cream of mushroom soup
1	(1.0-ounce) envelope dry onion soup mix
2	tablespoons cornstarch
2	tablespoons water

● Sprinkle roast with pepper; place in a 5-quart slow cooker. Add beef broth, cream of mushroom soup, and onion soup mix.

● Cover and cook on HIGH 1 hour. Reduce heat to LOW, and cook 7 hours or until tender. Transfer roast to a serving platter, reserving juices; keep warm.

● Whisk together cornstarch and water; slowly whisk into juices. Increase heat to HIGH, and cook, uncovered, 1 minute or until slightly thickened, whisking frequently. Serve roast with gravy. Makes 6 to 8 servings.

Slow-Cooker Size: 5-quart

Prep: 6 minutes
Cook: 8 hours, 1 minute

Sandwich Fixin's

Leftovers make great sandwiches. Just shred meat and spoon over toasted hoagies or bakery rolls.

Simple Mashed Potatoes

Using the paddle attachment with your stand mixer makes quick work of mashing the potatoes. Be sure not to overmix.

2½ pounds red potatoes
¼ cup butter
1 teaspoon salt
½ teaspoon pepper
¾ cup whipping cream
Garnish: pats of butter

Prep: 10 minutes
Cook: 35 minutes

Substitution Tip
Yukon gold or russet potatoes may be substituted.

● Bring potatoes and cold water to cover to a boil in a large Dutch oven; boil 25 minutes or until tender. Drain.
● Beat potatoes at low speed with an electric mixer just until mashed. Add ¼ cup butter, salt, and pepper, beating until butter is melted. Gradually add cream, beating just until smooth. Serve immediately. Garnish, if desired. Makes 6 servings.

Double Dip Party

serves 12

French Dip Sandwiches

potato chips   carrot sticks

Toffee Cappuccino Fondue

Toffee Cappuccino Fondue

This yummy coffee fondue tempts partygoers to dip the night away!

Slow-Cooker Size: 3-quart

Prep: 12 minutes
Cook: 1 hour

Leftover Delight

Reheat refrigerated leftover fondue in the microwave to serve as an ice cream topping.

1   (14-ounce) can sweetened condensed milk
1   (10-ounce) package almond toffee bits
½   cup fat-free caramel topping (we tested with Smuckers)
2   tablespoons instant coffee or espresso granules
1   (16-ounce) package vanilla bark coating, broken into chunks (we tested with Eagle Brand)
¼   cup dark chocolate morsels (we tested with Hershey's Special Dark Chocolate Chips)
Buttery cracker sticks (we tested with Ritz Cracker Sticks)

● Combine first 4 ingredients in a 3-quart slow cooker. Stir vanilla bark coating into milk mixture.
● Cover and cook on LOW 1 hour. Add chocolate morsels; stir fondue mixture until melted and smooth. Keep warm on LOW. Serve with cracker sticks. Makes 4 cups.

Company's Coming • 15 Minutes or Less to Prep

French Dip Sandwiches

1	(3½- to 4-pound) boneless chuck roast, trimmed and cut in half
½	cup soy sauce
1	beef bouillon cube
1	bay leaf
3	to 4 peppercorns, crushed
1	teaspoon dried rosemary, crushed
1	teaspoon dried thyme
1	teaspoon garlic powder
12	French sandwich rolls, split

Slow-Cooker Size: 5-quart

Prep: 5 minutes
Cook: 7 hours

Party Plan

Feel free to substitute smaller rolls to make bite-size sandwiches, if desired.

● Place roast in a 5-quart slow cooker. Combine soy sauce and next 6 ingredients; pour over roast. Add water to slow cooker until roast is almost covered.

● Cover and cook on LOW 7 hours or until very tender. Remove roast, reserving broth; shred roast with 2 forks. Place shredded meat evenly in rolls, and serve with reserved broth for dipping. Makes 12 servings.

Casual Fiesta

serves 10

Chunky Sausage Queso   *tortilla chips*

Blue Margaritas (double recipe)

taquitos   *guacamole salad*

5 Ingredients or Less

Chunky Sausage Queso

1   pound ground hot pork sausage
1   (16-ounce) jar processed cheese spread
1   (16-ounce) loaf pasteurized prepared
      cheese product, cubed
1   (20-ounce) jar hot salsa

● Brown sausage in a large skillet, stirring until it crumbles and is no longer pink; rinse and drain.
● Stir together sausage and remaining ingredients in a 2½-quart slow cooker. Cover and cook on LOW 2 hours or until cheese melts. Serve with tortilla chips. Makes 6 cups.

Slow-Cooker Size: 2½-quart

Prep: 15 minutes
Cook: 2 hours

Substitution Tip

If you prefer mild queso, use regular ground pork sausage instead of hot.

15 Minutes or Less to Prep

Blue Margaritas

1   (10-ounce) can frozen margarita mix
¾   cup tequila
¼   cup blue curaçao liqueur
2   tablespoons lime juice

● Combine all ingredients in a blender. Fill with ice to 5-cup level, and process until smooth. Serve immediately. Makes about 5 cups.

Prep: 5 minutes

Perfectly Sugared

For an even coating around the rim of each glass, first dip in lime juice and then in colored sugar.

Relishing the Grill

serves 6

Marinated Flank Steak   *Sweet Pepper Relish*

Cheesy Mashed Potatoes   *Mocha Pudding Cake (page 174)*

Slow-Cooker Size: 3-quart

Prep: 14 minutes
Cook: 7 hours
Other: 8 hours

Serving Suggestion

Use this versatile relish over roasted meats, poultry, and fish. It's also tasty for spicing up sandwiches, hamburgers, black-eyed peas, or cream cheese appetizers.

Editor's Favorite • 5 Ingredients or Less

Sweet Pepper Relish

2   red bell peppers, seeded and cut into thin strips
2   yellow bell peppers, seeded and cut into thin strips
¾   cup firmly packed brown sugar
8   serrano chile peppers, seeded and cut into thin strips

● Combine all ingredients in an airtight container. Cover and chill at least 8 hours.
● Spoon mixture into a lightly greased 3-quart slow cooker. Cover and cook on LOW 7 hours. Serve warm or cold. Makes 2½ cups.

Marinated Flank Steak

3 (2-pound) flank steaks
1 (12-ounce) can beer
1 (8-ounce) bottle Italian dressing
¼ to ⅓ cup fajita seasoning (we tested
with Bolner's Fiesta Brand)

- Place each flank steak in a large zip-top freezer bag. Combine beer, Italian dressing, and fajita seasoning; pour evenly over steaks. Seal bags, and chill 8 hours, turning occasionally.
- Remove steaks from marinade, discarding marinade. Prepare a hot fire by piling charcoal on one side of grill, leaving other side empty. (For gas grills, only light one side.) Place food grate on grill. Place steaks on lighted side of grill. Grill, covered with grill lid, over medium-high heat (350° to 400°) about 20 minutes or to desired degree of doneness. Let stand 10 minutes before slicing. Makes 12 servings.

Prep: 20 minutes
Cook: 20 minutes
Other: 8 hours, 10 minutes

Leftover Delight

Top a crisp green salad with leftover slices of steak for lunch the next day.

Cheesy Mashed Potatoes

2 pounds Yukon gold potatoes, peeled
and cubed
2 (5.2-ounce) packages buttery garlic-and-
herb spreadable cheese
⅔ cup half-and-half
¼ cup butter or margarine
¼ teaspoon salt
¼ teaspoon pepper

- Bring potato and water to cover to a boil in a large saucepan; reduce heat, and cook 15 to 20 minutes or until tender. Drain.
- Combine potato, cheese, and remaining ingredients in a large bowl; beat at medium speed with an electric mixer until smooth. Spoon into a lightly greased 2½-quart baking dish. Bake at 350° for 15 minutes or until top begins to brown. Makes 6 servings.

Prep: 35 minutes
Cook: 15 minutes

Test Kitchen Secret

Garnish these potatoes with fresh chopped thyme for taste and visual appeal.

Simple Ladies' Luncheon

serves 6

Peach Holiday Ham   marinated slaw

yeast rolls   lemonade

Cranberry Rice Pudding

Southern Classic

Peach Holiday Ham

1   (8-pound) smoked fully cooked ham
1   cup peach preserves
1   cup peach nectar
3   tablespoons coarse grained mustard
¼   teaspoon ground cloves

● Remove skin and excess fat from ham. Score fat on ham in a diamond pattern. Place the ham, fat side up, in a heavy-duty aluminum foil-lined roasting pan.
● Stir together peach preserves and remaining 3 ingredients; pour mixture evenly over ham.
● Bake at 325° for 1½ hours or until a meat thermometer inserted in ham registers 140°, basting every 20 minutes. Shield with foil after 30 minutes to prevent excess browning. Let stand 10 minutes before slicing. Makes 8 to 10 servings.

Prep: 25 minutes
Cook: 1 hour, 30 minutes
Other: 10 minutes

Leftover Delight

Serve leftover ham and rolls for a light lunch the next day.

Mustard gives
this sweet ham
savory charm.

Cranberry Rice Pudding

1½ cups uncooked instant brown rice
    (3¾ cups cooked; we tested with
    Uncle Ben's)
1   teaspoon ground cinnamon
¼   teaspoon salt
¼   teaspoon ground nutmeg
1   vanilla bean, split
1   (16-ounce) bottle hazelnut-flavored
    half-and-half (we tested with
    Coffeemate)
1   (14-ounce) can sweetened condensed
    milk
1   cup chopped hazelnuts, toasted
1   cup sweetened dried cranberries

● Cook rice according to package directions, using 1 tablespoon butter and ¾ teaspoon salt. Combine cooked rice and next 6 ingredients in a lightly greased 4-quart slow cooker.
● Cover and cook on HIGH 3½ hours or until thickened, stirring once. Remove vanilla bean; scrape seeds from inside bean, discarding bean. Stir vanilla seeds, hazelnuts, and cranberries into pudding. Serve warm or at room temperature. Makes 6 servings.

Slow-Cooker Size: 4-quart

Prep: 5 minutes
Cook: 3 hours, 30 minutes

Creamier

To ensure a creamy texture of this pudding, don't mistake hazelnut-flavored half-and-half with liquid creamer. Hazelnut half-and-half is not available everywhere, but regular Coffeemate half-and-half is. If using the latter as your substitution, also add ½ cup brown sugar and ¼ cup hazelnut liqueur for a comparable product.

Crockin' Around the Christmas Tree

serves 4

Stuffed Cornish Hens with Orange-Cranberry Sauce

Scalloped Potato Duo with Ham   Sautéed Brussels Sprouts with Chestnuts

Pumpkin Cheesecake

■■ ■ ■ ■ ■ ■ ■ ■ ■ ■ ■ ■ ■ ■ ■ ■ ■ ■

Company's Coming • 15 Minutes or Less to Prep

Stuffed Cornish Hens with Orange-Cranberry Sauce

Slow-Cooker Size: 5½- or
6-quart

Prep: 12 minutes
Cook: 7 hours

Party Plan

Cornish hens are ideal for a dinner party or special occasion. Aim for using hens no larger than 1¼ pounds each for the best fit in your slow cooker.

1   (6-ounce) package cornbread stuffing mix
1   tablespoon fresh lemon juice, divided
½   cup sweetened dried cranberries, chopped (we tested with Craisins)
⅓   cup chopped pecans, toasted
1   teaspoon minced fresh ginger
1   tablespoon grated orange rind
¾   cup orange marmalade
½   teaspoon salt
½   teaspoon coarsely ground pepper
4   (1¼-pound) Cornish hens

● Prepare stuffing mix according to package directions, omitting butter. Stir in 1 teaspoon lemon juice, dried cranberries, and next 3 ingredients.
● Combine marmalade, remaining 2 teaspoons lemon juice, salt, and pepper in a small microwave-safe bowl. Microwave at HIGH 1 minute or until marmalade is melted, stirring once.
● Spoon stuffing mixture evenly into hens. Place hens, stuffing sides up, in a 5½- or 6-quart slow cooker. Pour marmalade mixture over hens.
● Cover and cook on HIGH 1 hour. Reduce heat to LOW, and cook 5 to 6 hours or until hens are done. Makes 4 servings.

Scalloped Potato Duo with Ham

Two types of potato, nutty Gruyère cheese, and salty ham give this entrée unusual appeal.

1   medium onion
1   tablespoon vegetable oil
3   garlic cloves, finely chopped
2   sweet potatoes, peeled and cut into
      1/4-inch slices (about 1 1/2 pounds)
2   baking potatoes, peeled and cut into
      1/4-inch slices (about 1 1/2 pounds)
1/2 cup all-purpose flour
1   teaspoon salt
1/4 teaspoon pepper
2   cups chopped ham
2   cups (8 ounces) shredded Gruyère
      cheese, divided
1 3/4 cups whipping cream
2   tablespoons butter, cut into pieces

● Sauté onion in oil over medium-high heat 5 minutes. Add garlic; cook 30 seconds. Remove from heat, and set aside. Place potatoes in a large bowl.
● Combine flour, salt, and pepper; sprinkle over potatoes, tossing to coat. Arrange half of potato mixture in a greased 13- x 9-inch baking dish or 3-quart gratin dish. Top with onion, ham, and 1 cup cheese. Top with remaining potato mixture. Pour cream over potato mixture. Dot with butter, and cover with aluminum foil.
● Bake at 400° for 50 minutes. Uncover, top with remaining 1 cup cheese, and bake 20 more minutes or until potatoes are tender and cheese is browned. Let stand 10 minutes before serving. Makes 6 servings.

Prep: 20 minutes
Cook: 1 hour, 15 minutes
Other: 10 minutes

Double Duty

This dish eats like a meal. If you happen to have leftovers, reheat this potato duo the next day for lunch.

Sautéed Brussels Sprouts with Chestnuts

Prep: 10 minutes
Cook: 21 minutes

Wine Selection

Use Chardonnay or Sauvignon Blanc for the ⅓ cup dry white wine, and serve the rest at dinner.

1	teaspoon margarine
2	tablespoons minced shallots
1	garlic clove, minced
1	pound Brussels sprouts, trimmed and quartered
⅓	cup dry white wine
⅓	cup water
¾	cup cooked, shelled, and halved chestnuts (about ¾ pound in shells)
2	tablespoons chopped pecans
¼	teaspoon salt
¼	teaspoon pepper

● Melt margarine in a nonstick skillet over medium heat. Add shallots and garlic; sauté 2 minutes. Add sprouts; sauté 3 minutes. Add wine and water; bring to a boil. Cover; reduce heat. Simmer 10 minutes. Uncover; cook over medium heat 1 minute or until most of liquid is absorbed. Stir in remaining ingredients. Makes 5 servings.

Pumpkin Cheesecake

Pumpkin Cheesecake

1¼ cups gingersnap crumbs (25 to 30 cookies)
3 tablespoons butter or margarine, melted
3 (8-ounce) packages cream cheese, softened
1¼ cups granulated sugar, divided
1 tablespoon vanilla extract
6 large eggs, separated
2 (16-ounce) cans pumpkin
2 large eggs
1 cup whipping cream
1 tablespoon powdered sugar

● Combine gingersnap crumbs and butter; press into bottom and 1 inch up sides of a lightly greased 12-inch springform pan. Set aside.
● Beat cream cheese at medium speed with an electric mixer until smooth; add 1 cup granulated sugar and vanilla, beating until creamy. Stir in 6 egg yolks. Pour 2½ cups mixture into prepared crust; set aside.
● Add pumpkin and 2 eggs to remaining cream cheese mixture, stirring well; set aside.
● Beat egg whites at high speed until foamy. Add remaining ¼ cup granulated sugar, 1 tablespoon at a time, beating until stiff peaks form and sugar dissolves. Fold into pumpkin mixture; pour over cream cheese mixture in crust.
● Bake at 300° for 1½ hours. Turn oven off, and run a knife around edge of cheesecake to loosen. Let stand in oven with door partially open 1½ hours. Remove sides of pan; cover and chill cheesecake.
● Beat whipping cream and powdered sugar at high speed with an electric mixer until soft peaks form; spread on top of cheesecake. Makes 12 servings.

Prep: 30 minutes
Cook: 1 hour, 30 minutes
Other: 1 hour, 30 minutes

Make-Ahead Tip

Save time on Christmas day by making this cheesecake a day or two ahead. Top the cheesecake with whipped cream when ready to serve.

Lucky New Year's Menu

serves 8

New Year's Soup   *Jalapeño Cornbread*

Slice-and-Bake Chocolate Chip Shortbread

Pomegranate-Champagne Cocktail

━ ━ ━ ━ ━━━ ━ ━ ━━━━━━━━━━━ ━ ━ ━

Comfort Food • 15 Minutes or Less to Prep

New Year's Soup

Slow-Cooker Size: 6-quart

Prep: 12 minutes
Cook: 10 hours
Other: 8 hours

Lucky Combination

Making this recipe is a great way to use up that leftover holiday ham. It also combines good luck black-eyed peas and greens in one simple recipe.

1   (16-ounce) package dried black-eyed
      peas
3   (14-ounce) cans chicken broth
2   (14½-ounce) cans diced tomatoes with
      celery, onion, and green bell pepper
1   (10-ounce) can diced tomatoes and
      green chiles
1   large onion, chopped
2   cups diced cooked ham
¾   teaspoon salt
¾   teaspoon freshly ground black pepper
7   garlic cloves
1   (1-pound) package chopped fresh
      collard greens
Hot sauce

• Place peas in a 6-quart slow cooker. Cover with water 2 inches above beans; let soak 8 hours. Rinse and drain; return peas to slow cooker.
• Stir broth and next 7 ingredients into peas; add greens. Cover and cook on LOW 10 hours or until peas and greens are tender. Serve with hot sauce. Makes 8 servings.

Jalapeño Cornbread

1 cup self-rising cornmeal
½ teaspoon baking soda
¼ teaspoon salt
1½ cups (6 ounces) shredded Cheddar
     cheese
½ cup chopped onion
1 cup milk
3 tablespoons bacon drippings
1 teaspoon garlic powder
3 large eggs, lightly beaten
3 jalapeño peppers, seeded and chopped
1 (7-ounce) can sweet whole kernel corn,
     drained
1 (2-ounce) jar diced pimiento, drained

Prep: 10 minutes
Cook: 45 minutes

Alternative Use

Cornbread and greens are a match made in heaven for New Year's. But this cornbread also makes a colorful addition to the Christmas dinner table with its specks of green jalapeño and red pimiento.

● Combine first 3 ingredients in a large bowl; add Cheddar cheese and remaining 8 ingredients, stirring just until dry ingredients are moistened. Spoon batter into a greased 10-inch cast-iron skillet.
● Bake at 350° for 45 minutes or until golden. Cut into wedges. Makes 10 servings.

Slice-and-Bake Chocolate Chip Shortbread

Prep: 45 minutes
Cook: 12 minutes per batch
Other: 4 hours

Make-Ahead Tip

Once you shape the logs, they can be kept in the refrigerator up to 1 week or frozen up to a month.

1 cup butter, softened
¾ cup powdered sugar
1 cup (6-ounce package) semisweet chocolate morsels
2 teaspoons vanilla extract
2 cups all-purpose flour
¼ teaspoon baking powder
⅛ teaspoon salt

● Beat butter at medium speed with an electric mixer until creamy. Gradually add powdered sugar, beating until mixture is smooth. Stir in chocolate morsels and vanilla.
● Stir together flour, baking powder, and salt. Gradually add to butter mixture, beating at low speed until blended.
● Shape dough into 3 (10-inch) logs; wrap logs separately in wax paper, and chill 4 hours. Cut each log into 28 slices, and place slices 1 inch apart on lightly greased baking sheets.
● Bake at 350° for 10 to 12 minutes or until edges are golden. Cool on wire racks. Makes 7 dozen.

Pomegranate-Champagne Cocktail

Prep: 5 minutes

Sweet Treat

Turbinado is a raw, very coarse sugar with a mild brown sugar-like taste. It's located with other sugars in the grocery store.

1 turbinado sugar cube
2 tablespoons pomegranate juice
½ cup Champagne or sparkling wine, chilled

● Place sugar cube in a Champagne flute; add 2 tablespoons pomegranate juice and ½ cup Champagne. Serve immediately. Makes 1 serving.

sensational starters

Surprise family and friends with tempting
drinks and snacks from the slow cooker.

Warm Homemade Lemonade

4 cups water
3 cups fresh lemon juice (about 13 lemons)
1¾ to 2 cups sugar
¼ cup honey
Cinnamon sticks

● Combine first 4 ingredients in a 3- or 3½-quart slow cooker.
● Cover and cook on LOW 3 hours or until thoroughly heated. Whisk well before serving. Serve warm with cinnamon sticks. Makes 9 cups.

Slow-Cooker Size: 3- or 3½-quart

Prep: 12 minutes
Cook: 3 hours

Lemon Squeeze

We prefer the taste of fresh lemons, but if you don't want to do all that squeezing, substitute lemon juice from concentrate.

This lemonade **warms your heart** and reminds you of summertime.

Caramel Apple Cider

1   (64-ounce) bottle apple cider
⅓   cup caramel topping
½   teaspoon ground cinnamon
Fresh whipped cream
Ground cinnamon
Additional caramel topping

- Combine first 3 ingredients in a 3-quart slow cooker.
- Cover and cook on LOW 3 to 4 hours. Ladle into individual mugs, and dollop with whipped cream; sprinkle with cinnamon. Drizzle with additional caramel topping. Makes 8 cups.

Slow-Cooker Size: 3-quart

Prep: 5 minutes
Cook: 4 hours

Serving Solution

This cider is perfect for a party because it can be cooked and served out of the same dish.

This cider calls to mind the classic Halloween treat.

Spicy Tomato Warm-Up

1   (46-ounce) can spicy-hot vegetable juice
1   tablespoon beef bouillon granules
3   tablespoons lemon juice
1   tablespoon Worcestershire sauce
½   teaspoon hot sauce
⅛   teaspoon pepper

● Combine all ingredients in a 3- or 4-quart slow cooker.
● Cover and cook on LOW at least 2 hours. Keep warm in slow cooker until ready to serve. Makes 5¾ cups.

Slow-Cooker Size: 3- or 4-quart

Prep: 3 minutes
Cook: 2 hours

Adults Only

Add vodka to turn this beverage into a warm Bloody Mary.

This beverage is **nice and spicy.** If you like just a little spice, reduce or omit the hot sauce.

Spirited Hot Mocha

8   cups milk
1   cup (6-ounce package) semisweet
        chocolate mini-morsels or 6 (1-ounce)
        semisweet chocolate baking squares,
        chopped
½   cup powdered sugar
¼   cup instant coffee granules
1   cup brandy
Sweetened whipped cream (optional)
Grated semisweet chocolate (optional)

- Combine first 5 ingredients in a 4-quart slow cooker.
- Cover and cook on LOW 4 to 5 hours or until thoroughly heated and chocolate is melted, whisking after 2 hours. Whisk before serving. Serve with sweetened whipped cream and grated chocolate, if desired. Makes 10 cups.

Slow-Cooker Size: 4-quart

Prep: 2 minutes
Cook: 5 hours

Party Tip

Serve this spiked favorite straight from the slow cooker.

Brandy adds a spirited punch to this coffee-flavored hot chocolate, but you can omit it, if desired.

Cranberry Spiced Wine

1   (3-inch) cinnamon stick
10   whole cloves
2   cups cranberry juice
½   cup orange juice
½   cup water
½   cup sugar
1   tablespoon lemon juice
1   (25.4-ounce) bottle dry red wine
      (we tested with Merlot)

• Combine first 7 ingredients in a 4- or 5-quart slow cooker.
• Cover and cook on LOW 4 hours. Stir in wine; cover and cook on LOW 30 more minutes or until thoroughly heated. Remove and discard cloves and cinnamon stick before serving. Makes 6 cups.

Slow-Cooker Size: 4- or 5-quart

Prep: 3 minutes
Cook: 4 hours, 30 minutes

Test Kitchen Secret

We used a cinnamon stick instead of ground cinnamon to avoid clouding the rose-colored beverage.

Spark the holiday spirit with this spiced combo of red wine and three juices.

Hot Parmesan-Artichoke Dip

1½ cups mayonnaise
2   (12-ounce) jars marinated quartered
      artichoke hearts, drained and chopped
2   (4.5-ounce) cans chopped green chiles,
      drained
1   (7-ounce) jar roasted red bell peppers,
      drained and chopped
2   cups freshly shredded Parmesan cheese
4   garlic cloves, minced
Toasted baguette slices or assorted crackers

● Stir together first 6 ingredients. Spoon into a 3-quart slow cooker.
● Cover and cook on LOW 4 hours. Stir well before serving. Serve with baguette slices or assorted crackers. Makes 6 cups.

Slow-Cooker Size: 3-quart

Prep: 18 minutes
Cook: 4 hours

Test Kitchen Secret

Freshly shredded Parmesan cheese melts more smoothly than preshredded options.

When it's
time to invite friends
and family over, make this
time-honored oven favorite
in the slow cooker!

Beer-and-Cheddar Fondue

Slow-Cooker Size: 3- or 4-quart

Prep: 20 minutes
Cook: 1 hour

Nonalcoholic

Substitute nonalcoholic beer for regular beer if you prefer an alcohol-free version of this fondue.

½ pound ground hot pork sausage
6 tablespoons butter
1½ cups chopped onion
1 garlic clove, chopped
6 tablespoons all-purpose flour
1 cup milk
2 (8-ounce) blocks Cheddar cheese, shredded
2 tablespoons all-purpose flour
1 cup dark beer
1 (4.5-ounce) can chopped green chiles, undrained
½ teaspoon salt
¼ teaspoon ground red pepper

● Cook sausage in a large saucepan over medium heat, stirring until it crumbles and is no longer pink. Drain and remove sausage from saucepan.
● Melt butter in saucepan over medium heat; add onion and garlic, and sauté until tender.
● Add 6 tablespoons flour, stirring until smooth. Cook, stirring constantly, 1 minute. Gradually add milk, stirring until thickened.
● Toss cheese lightly with 2 tablespoons flour. Add cheese mixture to milk mixture, stirring until blended. Transfer to a 3- or 4-quart slow cooker; stir in sausage, beer, and remaining ingredients.
● Cover and cook on LOW 1 hour. Serve with cubed French bread or sliced pears. Makes about 6 cups.

Slow-Cooker Queso Blanco

Buy white American cheese by the pound at the deli counter to make this addictive dip. Have the cheese sliced at the deli so you can forgo shredding it; then just roughly tear the slices and place them in the slow cooker.

1   small onion, diced
3   garlic cloves, minced
1   (14½-ounce) can petite cut diced
    tomatoes, drained
1   cup milk
¾   cup pickled jalapeño slices, minced
1   tablespoon juice from jalapeño slices
1   (4.5-ounce) can chopped green chiles,
    undrained
1   teaspoon ground cumin
½   teaspoon dried oregano
½   teaspoon coarsely ground pepper
2   pounds deli white American cheese,
    sliced (we tested with DiLusso)

● Place onion in a medium-size microwave-safe bowl; cover loosely with heavy-duty plastic wrap. Microwave at HIGH 2 minutes. Stir in garlic and next 8 ingredients.
● Roughly tear cheese slices; place in a 4-quart slow cooker. Pour onion mixture over cheese.
● Cover and cook on LOW 2 hours. Stir gently to blend ingredients. Serve with tortilla chips. Makes 6½ cups.

Slow-Cooker Size: 4-quart

Prep: 22 minutes
Cook: 2 hours

Freeze It!

This queso dip freezes well. Spoon into serving-size freezer containers, and freeze up to 1 month. Thaw overnight in refrigerator. Reheat in microwave at MEDIUM.

This creamy queso rivals any served at Mexican restaurants.

Baked Pimiento Cheese Dip

This irresistibly cheesy dip is great with celery sticks or crackers or even as a topping for baked potatoes, open-faced tomato sandwiches, or hot brown sandwiches.

Slow-Cooker Size: 3-quart

Prep: 17 minutes
Cook: 3 hours

Updated Classic

The addition of cornstarch to classic pimiento cheese helps to keep the oil from separating when the dip is heated. You may want to give the dip a quick stir before serving.

1 (10-ounce) block sharp Cheddar cheese, shredded (we tested with Cracker Barrel)
1 (10-ounce) block extra-sharp Cheddar cheese, shredded (we tested with Cracker Barrel)
1 tablespoon cornstarch
8 bacon slices, cooked and crumbled
½ small onion, finely grated (about 3 tablespoons)
1 cup mayonnaise
2 (4-ounce) jars diced pimiento, drained
2 teaspoons Worcestershire sauce
¼ teaspoon pepper

● Toss together cheeses and cornstarch in a medium bowl. Add half of bacon and all of remaining ingredients; stir well to blend. Spoon mixture into a lightly greased 3-quart slow cooker. Sprinkle with remaining bacon.
● Cover and cook on LOW 2 to 3 hours or until melted and bubbly. Serve warm with crackers. Makes 5 cups.

Reuben Spread

½ pound sliced deli corned beef,
     coarsely chopped
1 cup sauerkraut, drained and chopped
1 teaspoon cider vinegar
¼ teaspoon caraway seeds
¼ teaspoon pepper
1 (8-ounce) package cream cheese,
     softened
½ cup Thousand Island dressing
2 cups shredded Swiss cheese

● Stir together first 7 ingredients and 1 cup Swiss cheese; spoon into a lightly greased 2- or 3-quart slow cooker. Top with remaining 1 cup cheese.
● Cover and cook on LOW 2 to 3 hours. Serve with rye Melba rounds or pretzel rods. Makes 3½ cups.

Slow-Cooker Size: 2- or 3-quart

Prep: 10 minutes
Cook: 3 hours

Test Kitchen Secret

Use kitchen shears to snip the sauerkraut into manageable pieces for a dip.

Rye melba rounds make fitting dippers for this spread that pays tribute to the sandwich for which it's named.

Creamy Dried Beef Dip

Dried beef tends to be salty, so be sure to use garlic powder instead of garlic salt in this recipe.

2 (8-ounce) packages cream cheese, softened
1 (8-ounce) container sour cream
¼ cup milk
¼ teaspoon garlic powder
¼ teaspoon black pepper
1 (4.5-ounce) jar dried beef, chopped
½ cup chopped green or red bell pepper
¼ cup finely chopped onion
½ cup chopped pecans

• Beat first 5 ingredients at medium speed with an electric mixer until blended; stir in beef and remaining ingredients. Spoon into a lightly greased 3-quart slow cooker.
• Cover and cook on LOW 3 hours. Stir before serving. Serve with bagel chips and red pepper strips. Makes 3¾ cups.

Add extra color
to this dip by using both green and red bell peppers.

Buffalo Chicken-Cheese Dip

Slow-Cooker Size: 2- or 3-quart

Prep: 5 minutes
Cook: 3 hours

Tailgating Tip

Hot cheese dip with the flavors of buffalo wings makes for an ideal tailgating treat. Bring lots of celery sticks, and watch this dip disappear!

1   tablespoon vegetable oil
1   onion, chopped
3   cups shredded cooked chicken
¾   to 1 cup hot sauce (we tested with Frank's)
1   (8-ounce) package cream cheese, softened
2   cups (8 ounces) shredded Cheddar cheese, divided
Celery sticks

● Heat oil in a nonstick skillet over medium-high heat. Add onion, and cook 4 minutes or until onion is tender.
● Combine onion, chicken, hot sauce, cream cheese, and 1 cup Cheddar cheese in a 2- or 3-quart slow cooker.
● Cover and cook on LOW 2½ hours. Remove lid; sprinkle top with remaining 1 cup Cheddar cheese. Cover and cook on LOW 30 more minutes or until cheese melts. Serve with celery sticks. Makes 5½ cups.

Enjoy the taste of
hot wings—without
getting your fingers messy.

Artichoke and Crabmeat Dip

2 (6-ounce) cans lump crabmeat, drained and picked
2 (14-ounce) cans quartered artichoke hearts, drained and chopped
4 garlic cloves, minced
¼ cup lemon juice
4 teaspoons hot sauce
½ cup shredded Parmesan cheese
2 (8-ounce) packages cream cheese, softened
¼ teaspoon white pepper
1 cup mini bagel chips, coarsely crushed

● Combine first 8 ingredients. Spoon into a lightly greased 3-quart slow cooker.
● Cover and cook on LOW 2½ hours. Stir until cheese is smooth; sprinkle with crushed bagel chips. Serve with bagel chips or pita chips. Makes 6 cups.

Slow-Cooker Size: 3-quart

Prep: 11 minutes
Cook: 2 hours, 30 minutes

Test Kitchen Secret

Pick through the crabmeat to remove fine cartilage if you like, but take care to leave the prized chunks of lump crabmeat intact as much as possible.

Creamy cheeses flecked with lump crabmeat create a **hearty** start for a party.

Sina's Georgia-Style Boiled Peanuts

Southern boiled peanuts are easily made in your slow cooker. They typically take all day on the stovetop, but now you can start them before bed and have them ready for tailgating the next afternoon.

2   pounds raw peanuts, in shell
¾   to 1 cup salt
12   cups water

● Combine all ingredients in a 5- or 6-quart slow cooker. Cover and cook on HIGH 18 hours or until peanuts are soft. Drain peanuts before serving or storing. Store in zip-top plastic bags in refrigerator up to 2 weeks. Makes 18 cups.

Cajun Boiled Peanuts: Add 1 (3-ounce) package boil-in-bag shrimp and crab boil and ⅓ to ½ cup hot sauce (we tested with Frank's) to slow cooker before cooking.

Slow-Cooker Size: 5- or 6-quart

Prep: 3 minutes
Cook: 18 hours

Freeze It!

Freeze these peanuts in zip-top freezer bags up to 2 months. Reheat them in the microwave before serving.

Lick your lips these
Southern peanuts
are salty goodness for
fall football games.

Chicken Wings with Spicy Chili Sauce

Slow-Cooker Size: 3-quart

Prep: 10 minutes
Cook: 4 hours, 8 minutes
Other: 8 hours

Spicy!

The spiciness of this appetizer varies depending on the brand of chili garlic sauce used.

2½ pounds chicken wings (about 13 wings)
¾ cup maple syrup
½ cup chili garlic sauce
      (we tested with Tuong Ot Toi)
1   small onion, diced
2   tablespoons Dijon mustard
2   teaspoons Worcestershire sauce
Celery sticks

● Cut off wingtips, and discard; cut wings in half at joint.
● Combine syrup and next 4 ingredients in a small bowl; reserve ¾ cup marinade, and refrigerate. Pour remaining marinade into a large zip-top freezer bag; add chicken and seal. Refrigerate 8 hours, turning bag occasionally.
● Remove chicken from marinade; discard marinade. Place chicken, skin sides up, on a lightly greased rack in a broiler pan. Broil, 3 inches from heat, 8 minutes or until browned.
● Place wings in a 3-quart slow cooker. Cover and cook on LOW 4 hours. Serve with reserved ¾ cup marinade and celery sticks. Makes 6 to 8 appetizer servings.

Maple syrup adds a
touch of sweetness
to this spicy chili sauce.

Spicy Sausage-Stuffed Mushrooms

½ pound hot ground pork sausage
½ (8-ounce) package cream cheese, softened
¼ teaspoon garlic powder
¼ teaspoon hot sauce
½ pound large fresh mushrooms (about 17 mushrooms)

- Cook sausage in a skillet over medium-high heat, stirring until it crumbles and is no longer pink. Drain sausage, and return to skillet.
- Reduce heat to medium; add cream cheese, garlic powder, and hot sauce, stirring until cheese melts. Remove from heat; cool slightly.
- Clean mushrooms with damp paper towels. Remove stems, and reserve for another use.
- Spoon sausage mixture evenly into mushroom caps. Place stuffed mushrooms in a single layer in a 6-quart oval slow cooker. Cover and cook on LOW 2 hours or until mushrooms are tender. Makes 8 or 9 appetizer servings.

Slow-Cooker Size: oval 6-quart

Prep: 13 minutes
Cook: 2 hours

Clean as a Whistle

Clean mushrooms with damp paper towels instead of washing them under running water to keep them from getting waterlogged.

Slow cooking stuffed mushrooms minimizes last-minute preparation and frees up your oven for other recipes.

soups & stews

Warm heart and soul with these
savory soups and chunky stews.

Pinto Bean Chili with Corn and Winter Squash

Slow-Cooker Size: 5-quart

Prep: 13 minutes
Cook: 8 hours

Know Your Cheese

Queso fresco is a crumbly, slightly salty Mexican cheese that's available in many large supermarkets. If you can't find it, substitute crumbled feta or farmer cheese.

2½ cups peeled and ½-inch-cubed butternut
　　squash (about 1 pound)
1　medium onion, chopped (about 1 cup)
1　red bell pepper, chopped (about ¾ cup)
1　garlic clove, minced
2　tablespoons chili powder
1　teaspoon salt
½　teaspoon ground cumin
2　(16-ounce) cans pinto beans, rinsed and
　　drained
1　(16-ounce) package frozen whole kernel
　　corn, thawed
1　(15-ounce) can crushed tomatoes
1　(4.5-ounce) can chopped green chiles
1½ cups water
¾　cup (3 ounces) crumbled queso fresco
Lime wedges

● Combine first 7 ingredients in a 5-quart slow cooker; add pinto beans and next 4 ingredients.
● Cover and cook on LOW 8 hours or until slightly thickened and squash is tender. Sprinkle with cheese before serving. Serve with lime wedges. Makes 9 cups.

The **spiciness** of this light yet satisfying chili is complemented by the subtle **sweetness** of corn and winter squash.

Steak-and-Black Bean Chili

2 tablespoons vegetable oil
2 pounds boneless top sirloin steak, cubed
3 (15-ounce) cans black beans
2 (10-ounce) cans chili-style diced
    tomatoes with green chiles, undrained
    (we tested with Rotel Chili Fixin's)
1 (10-ounce) package frozen chopped
    onion, thawed
1 green bell pepper, chopped
4 garlic cloves, minced
1 (12-ounce) bottle dark beer
1 cup water
2 tablespoons chili powder
1 tablespoon ground cumin
1 teaspoon salt
1 teaspoon sugar
Toppings: shredded Cheddar cheese, sliced
    green onions, sour cream, chopped
    jalapeño peppers, dried tomatoes

- Heat oil in a large skillet over high heat. Add steak; cook 3 to 4 minutes, stirring constantly, or until browned.
- Place steak in a 6-quart slow cooker; stir in black beans and next 10 ingredients.
- Cover and cook on LOW 8 hours. Serve with desired toppings. Makes 14 cups.

Slow-Cooker Size: 6-quart

Prep: 10 minutes
Cook: 8 hours

Make-Ahead Tip

To cook this chili ahead, set up your slow cooker right before bedtime, and the chili will be ready the next morning. Let it cool; then cover and refrigerate it until you're ready to reheat it.

Big-Batch Chili

4   pounds ground chuck
2   medium onions, chopped
1   green bell pepper, chopped
2   garlic cloves, minced
3   (14½-ounce) cans diced tomatoes, undrained
4   (8-ounce) cans tomato sauce
1   (6-ounce) can tomato paste
¼   cup chili powder
1   tablespoon sugar
1   teaspoon salt
1   teaspoon black pepper
½   teaspoon paprika
½   teaspoon ground red pepper
1   bay leaf
2   (16-ounce) cans light red kidney beans, rinsed and drained (optional)
Toppings: sour cream, shredded Cheddar cheese, chopped green onions, sliced ripe black olives

● Cook ground chuck, in batches, in a large skillet over medium-high heat about 5 minutes, stirring until it crumbles and is no longer pink; drain.
● Place meat in a 6-quart slow cooker; stir in onion, next 12 ingredients, and, if desired, beans.
● Cover and cook on HIGH 5 to 6 hours or on LOW 7 to 8 hours. Remove and discard bay leaf. Serve with desired toppings. Makes 15 to 18 cups.

Slow-Cooker Size: 6-quart

Prep: 20 minutes
Cook: 6 hours or 8 hours

Freeze It!

Let chili cool before freezing. Evenly divide chili into 3 (1-gallon) zip-top freezer bags; seal and lay each bag flat. Stack bags of chili in freezer. Freeze up to 1 month. Thaw 1 bag of frozen chili overnight in refrigerator, or defrost in microwave. Pour thawed chili into a 9-inch square baking dish. Cover tightly with heavy-duty plastic wrap, and fold back a corner to allow steam to escape. Microwave at HIGH 6 to 7 minutes or until bubbly, stirring after 3½ minutes.

South-of-the-Border Corn Chowder

3 large potatoes, peeled and cut into
   ½-inch cubes (about 1¾ pounds)
1 (16-ounce) package frozen whole kernel
   corn, thawed
2 (14-ounce) cans chicken broth
2 celery ribs, chopped
1 jalapeño pepper, minced
1 tablespoon minced garlic
1½ tablespoons chili powder
1½ teaspoons salt
1 cup whipping cream
Toppings: cooked and crumbled bacon,
   shredded Cheddar cheese, crushed
   corn chips

Slow-Cooker Size: 4-quart

Prep: 16 minutes
Cook: 8 hours

Spicy!

If you prefer milder flavors, feel free to omit the jalapeño pepper.

- Combine first 8 ingredients in a 4-quart slow cooker.
- Cover and cook on LOW 8 hours or until potatoes are tender.
- Stir in cream. Using a potato masher, partially mash potatoes in slow cooker until chowder is desired consistency. Serve with desired toppings. Makes 10 cups.

Here's the perfect beginning
for any fiesta.

Hoppin' John Chowder

- 4 (15.8-ounce) cans black-eyed peas, undrained
- 2 (10-ounce) cans diced tomatoes and green chiles, undrained
- 1 (14-ounce) can beef broth
- 1 pound smoked sausage, sliced
- 1 cup water
- 1 cup finely chopped onion
- ¾ cup chopped green bell pepper
- ½ teaspoon garlic powder
- ¼ teaspoon salt
- ¼ teaspoon black pepper
- 1 family-size package boil-in-bag rice, uncooked (about 1½ cups uncooked)

- Combine all ingredients except rice in a 6-quart slow cooker.
- Cover and cook on LOW 6 hours. Cut top off boil-in-bag rice; pour rice into slow cooker, and discard bag. Stir.
- Cover and cook on HIGH 20 minutes or until rice is tender. Makes 18 cups.

Slow-Cooker Size: 6-quart

Prep: 14 minutes
Cook: 6 hours, 20 minutes

Rice Is Nice

Adding quick-cooking boil-in-bag rice at the end of the cooking keeps the rice tender and prevents overcooking.

This twist on a Southern favorite includes smoked sausage to make it even heartier. Serve it with warm crusty French bread for soppin' up juices.

Tomato Florentine Soup

3   cups chicken broth
2   (14½-ounce) cans diced tomatoes with
       basil, oregano, and garlic, undrained
1   (15-ounce) can tomato sauce
1   (10-ounce) package frozen chopped
       spinach, thawed and well drained
1   cup chopped onion
1½ teaspoons minced garlic
½   teaspoon salt
¼   teaspoon pepper
1   (9-ounce) package refrigerated
       cheese-filled tortellini
Garnish: shredded Parmesan cheese

● Combine first 8 ingredients in a 4-quart slow cooker.
● Cover and cook on LOW 5½ hours; add pasta, and cook
on LOW 30 more minutes. Garnish with Parmesan cheese,
if desired. Makes 10 cups.

Slow-Cooker Size: 4-quart

Prep: 4 minutes
Cook: 6 hours

Quick Menu
● Grilled cheese sandwich
● Iced tea

Serve this light and flavorful tomato soup with a grilled cheese sandwich for a hearty winter lunch.

"Baked" Potato Soup

Slow-Cooker Size: 5-quart

Prep: 21 minutes
Cook: 4 hours or 8 hours

Lighten Up

Reduce the fat in this soup by using fat-free half-and-half along with reduced-fat cheese and sour cream.

6	large russet potatoes, peeled and cut into ½-inch cubes (about 3¾ pounds)
1	large onion, chopped (about 1½ cups)
3	(14-ounce) cans chicken broth with roasted garlic
¼	cup butter
2½	teaspoons salt
1¼	teaspoons freshly ground pepper
1	cup whipping cream or half-and-half
1	cup (4 ounces) sharp Cheddar cheese, shredded
3	tablespoons chopped fresh chives
1	(8-ounce) container sour cream (optional)
4	bacon slices, cooked and crumbled

Shredded Cheddar cheese

● Combine first 6 ingredients in a 5-quart slow cooker.
● Cover and cook on HIGH 4 hours or on LOW 8 hours or until potato is tender.
● Mash mixture until potatoes are coarsely chopped and soup is slightly thickened; stir in cream, cheese, and chives. Top with sour cream, if desired, and sprinkle with bacon and Cheddar cheese before serving. Makes 12 cups.

Consider this the **down-home comfort** version of a loaded twice-baked potato—warm and creamy, just the way potato soup should be.

Southern Sweet Potato Soup

- 2 large sweet potatoes, peeled and sliced (about 2 pounds)
- 2 (14-ounce) cans chicken broth
- 3 cups chopped onion
- 2 celery ribs, chopped (about 1 cup)
- 2 garlic cloves, minced
- ½ cup water
- ⅓ cup butter, melted
- 3 tablespoons creamy peanut butter
- 1 cinnamon stick
- 2 cups whipping cream
- ¾ teaspoon salt
- 1 tablespoon chopped fresh thyme
- ½ cup whipping cream
- 1½ tablespoons molasses
- ⅛ teaspoon salt
- ⅛ teaspoon ground nutmeg
- Lime wedges
- Garnish: chopped dry-roasted peanuts

- Combine first 9 ingredients in a 5-quart slow cooker.
- Cover and cook on LOW 7 hours or until potatoes are tender. Remove and discard cinnamon stick. Cool soup slightly.
- Process soup, in batches, in a food processor until smooth.
- Return soup to slow cooker. Add 2 cups whipping cream, ¾ teaspoon salt, and thyme.
- Cover and cook on HIGH 30 to 45 minutes or until thoroughly heated.
- Combine ½ cup whipping cream, molasses, ⅛ teaspoon salt, and nutmeg in a small bowl; beat at medium speed with an electric mixer until soft peaks form. Serve soup with whipped cream and a lime wedge; garnish, if desired. Makes 10 cups.

Slow-Cooker Size: 5-quart

Prep: 22 minutes
Cook: 7 hours, 45 minutes

Broth Swap

We liked the flavor of chicken broth in this meatless delight. If you're looking for a vegetarian soup, substitute vegetable broth instead.

Portobello Mushroom Soup

2   tablespoons olive oil
2   (8-ounce) packages sliced fresh baby portobello mushrooms, coarsely chopped
1   medium onion, chopped
1   garlic clove, minced
2   (14-ounce) cans beef broth
¼   cup dry sherry
1   tablespoon tomato paste
1   tablespoon chopped fresh thyme
1   tablespoon Worcestershire sauce
½   teaspoon salt
½   to ¾ teaspoon pepper
1   (12-ounce) can evaporated milk
2   tablespoons all-purpose flour

● Heat oil in a large skillet over medium-high heat. Add mushrooms, onion, and garlic. Sauté 3 to 5 minutes or until vegetables are tender.
● Transfer vegetables to a 6-quart slow cooker; add broth and next 6 ingredients.
● Cover and cook on LOW 4 hours.
● Whisk together milk and flour; stir into soup.
● Cover and cook on LOW 30 more minutes. Makes 8 cups.

This soup is creamy without being too heavy. It makes an ideal summertime soup.

Spicy Cabbage-Beef Soup

1   pound ground round
1   small head cabbage, cut into 1-inch
      pieces (about 5 cups)
1   medium onion, chopped (about 1 cup)
1   (16-ounce) kidney beans
1   (15-ounce) can crushed tomatoes
1   (14-ounce) can beef broth
1   (10-ounce) can diced tomatoes and
      green chiles, undrained
1   teaspoon salt
1   teaspoon ground cumin
½   teaspoon pepper
¼   teaspoon dried oregano

● Brown beef in a large nonstick skillet, stirring until it crumbles and is no longer pink. Drain.
● Place cabbage in a 4-quart slow cooker. Combine beef, onion, and remaining 8 ingredients; add to slow cooker.
● Cover and cook on HIGH 6 hours or until cabbage is tender. Makes 12 cups.

Slow-Cooker Size: 4-quart

Prep: 8 minutes
Cook: 6 hours

Spicy!

You can spice up this comforting dish using extra-hot diced tomatoes and green chiles.

Beefy Bello Soup

2 pounds beef stew meat
¼ cup all-purpose flour
3 tablespoons olive oil, divided
1 large onion, chopped
2 celery ribs, thinly sliced
3 garlic cloves, pressed
2 (14-ounce) cans beef broth
1 (8-ounce) package sliced fresh baby
   portobello mushrooms
2 tablespoons fresh thyme leaves
1 teaspoon salt
1 teaspoon freshly ground black pepper

● Combine beef and flour in a large zip-top plastic bag; shake well to coat.

● Heat 1 tablespoon oil in a large nonstick skillet over medium-high heat. Add half of beef, and cook 4 minutes or until browned on all sides. Repeat with 1 tablespoon oil and remaining beef. Transfer browned beef to a 4-quart slow cooker.

● Heat remaining 1 tablespoon oil over medium-high heat in skillet. Add onion, celery, and garlic; cook 4 minutes or until almost tender. Add vegetable mixture to slow cooker. Add broth and remaining ingredients.

● Cover and cook on LOW 8 hours or until beef is tender. Makes 8 cups.

Slow-Cooker Size: 4-quart

Prep: 9 minutes
Cook: 8 hours

Serving Suggestion

This hearty soup satisfies and impresses your hungriest guest. Serve it with a mixed green salad and crusty French bread for savoring the broth.

Steak Soup

This soup does not freeze well, so halve the recipe if you can't make use of the entire batch in two or three days.

1	(2-pound) package top round steak, cut into 1-inch cubes
⅓	cup all-purpose flour
3	tablespoons vegetable oil
4	cups water
5	baking potatoes, cut into ½-inch cubes
3	carrots, sliced
2	small onions, chopped
1	celery rib, chopped
1	cup frozen sweet peas
1	(15.25-ounce) can whole kernel corn, drained
1	(6-ounce) can tomato paste
2	tablespoons beef bouillon granules
1	to 2 teaspoons pepper

● Combine beef and flour in a large zip-top plastic bag; shake well to coat.
● Brown steak in hot oil in a large skillet over medium-high heat 5 to 6 minutes.
● Stir together steak, 4 cups water, and remaining ingredients in a 5-quart slow cooker.
● Cover and cook on **HIGH** 8 hours or until steak and vegetables are tender. Makes 16 cups.

Slow-Cooker Size: 5-quart

Prep: 30 minutes
Cook: 8 hours

Party Plan

Throw a football party and serve this chunky, comforting soup. Offer fun toppings, such as fresh tomatoes, Cheddar cheese, sour cream, and crumbled tortilla or corn chips.

Loaded with meat and veggies, this chunky soup is a meal in one dish.

Taco Soup

Slow-Cooker Size: 5½-quart

Prep: 15 minutes
Cook: 6 hours

Non alcoholic

Use alcohol-free beer instead of regular, if you prefer.

1½ pounds ground beef
1   cup chopped red onion
1   (1.25-ounce) package taco seasoning
     mix
1   (1-ounce) envelope Ranch-style
     dressing mix
2   (15.25-ounce) cans whole kernel corn,
     undrained
1   (16-ounce) can pinto beans, undrained
1   (15-ounce) can black beans, undrained
2   (10-ounce) cans chili-style diced
     tomatoes with green chiles, undrained
     (we tested with Rotel Chili Fixin's)
1   (12-ounce) can light beer
1½ cups water
Toppings: shredded Cheddar cheese, sour
     cream, tortilla chips, cilantro

• Cook beef and onion in a large skillet over medium-high heat, stirring until meat crumbles and is no longer pink; drain.
• Combine meat mixture, taco seasoning mix, and next 7 ingredients in a 5½-quart slow cooker.
• Cover and cook on LOW 5 to 6 hours. Serve with desired toppings. Makes 16 cups.

This is a
clear-out-the-cupboard
soup that the whole family
will enjoy.

Sausage and Lentil Soup

1   pound smoked sausage, sliced
¾   pound dried lentils, rinsed and drained
      (1¾ cups)
1   cup diced ham
1   medium onion, chopped
1   small green bell pepper, chopped
      (¾ cup)
1   medium carrot, diced (¾ cup)
2   large garlic cloves, minced
½   teaspoon dried thyme
¼   teaspoon pepper
¼   teaspoon ground cumin
1   bay leaf
2   (14-ounce) cans beef broth
2   (14-ounce) cans chicken broth
2   cups coarsely chopped fresh spinach

• Combine all ingredients except spinach in a 5-quart slow cooker.
• Cover and cook on LOW 6 hours or until lentils are tender.
• Add spinach; cover and let stand 5 minutes or until spinach wilts. Remove and discard bay leaf. Makes 12 cups.

Slow-Cooker Size: 5-quart

Prep: 20 minutes
Cook: 6 hours
Other: 5 minutes

Make Mine Spicy

If you want to kick up the heat a little, use spicy smoked sausage in place of regular.

Quick Menu

• Waldorf salad
• Corn muffins

Wilted spinach adds
incredible texture
to this robust soup.

15-Bean Soup with Ham

1 (20-ounce) package dried 15-bean soup
  mix (we tested with Ham Been)
6 bacon slices
1 large onion, chopped
2 large carrots, sliced
2 celery ribs, sliced
5 garlic cloves, pressed
1 (12-ounce) package diced cooked ham
  (about 2 cups; we tested with Hormel)
1 (32-ounce) container chicken broth
2 (14.5-ounce) cans stewed tomatoes with
  onion, celery, and green bell pepper
2 teaspoons dry mustard
1 teaspoon salt
1 teaspoon freshly ground black pepper
½ teaspoon ground red pepper

● Place beans in a 6-quart slow cooker. Cover with water 2 inches above beans; let soak 8 hours. Drain and rinse; return beans to slow cooker.

● Cook bacon in a large skillet until crisp; remove bacon, and drain on paper towels, reserving 1 tablespoon drippings in skillet. Crumble bacon, and set aside.

● Sauté onion and next 3 ingredients in hot drippings in skillet until onion is lightly browned and tender; add to slow cooker. Stir in ham and remaining 6 ingredients.

● Cover and cook on LOW 10 hours or until beans are tender. Sprinkle each serving with bacon. Makes 9 cups.

Slow-Cooker Size: 6-quart

Prep: 13 minutes
Cook: 10 hours
Other: 8 hours

Leftover Ham Fixin's

Nothing beats the smoky flavor of a holiday ham. And what better way to use the leftovers than in bean and ham soup? Instead of using a package of diced ham, just dice 2 cups leftover ham, throw the ham into the slow cooker, and get ready for a cozy evening meal.

Broccoli, Ham, and Cheese Soup

Slow-Cooker Size: 5-quart

Prep: 15 minutes
Cook: 8 hours, 30 minutes

Kids in the Kitchen

Your children will beg for more of this cheesy concoction. Let them help by adding ingredients to the slow cooker.

5   large russet potatoes, peeled and cubed
4   garlic cloves, pressed
1   medium onion, chopped
2   (14-ounce) cans chicken broth
1   (12-ounce) package diced cooked ham
      (about 2 cups; we tested with Hormel)
1½ cups broccoli florets
½   teaspoons salt
¾   teaspoon pepper
2   cups whipping cream
2   cups (8 ounces) shredded sharp Cheddar
      cheese
Toppings: sour cream, shredded Cheddar
      cheese

- Combine first 8 ingredients in a 5-quart slow cooker.
- Cover and cook on LOW 8 hours or until potatoes are tender.
- Process half of soup mixture in a food processor until smooth. Gradually stir potato puree, whipping cream, and 2 cups cheese into remaining soup mixture.
- Cover and cook on LOW 30 more minutes or until thoroughly heated. Serve with desired toppings. Makes 12 cups.

It's a cinch to get kids to eat their broccoli with this rich cheese soup.

Ham-and-White Bean Soup

1 (16-ounce) package dried great
  Northern beans
1 large sweet onion, chopped
3 garlic cloves, minced
1 teaspoon dried crushed red pepper
1 smoked ham hock or ham bone
3 cups chopped cooked ham
4 (14-ounce) cans chicken broth

- Place beans in a 6-quart slow cooker. Cover with water 2 inches above beans. Let soak 8 hours. Drain and rinse; return beans to slow cooker.
- Sprinkle onion, garlic, and red pepper over beans. Place ham hock in center of beans, pressing it to the bottom of slow cooker. Sprinkle chopped ham over beans; pour broth over ham.
- Cover and cook on HIGH 1 hour.
- Reduce heat to LOW, and cook 8 hours. Uncover and mash some of the beans with the back of a large spoon or potato masher.
- Cover and cook on LOW 1 more hour. Stir well before serving. Makes 12 cups.

Slow-Cooker Size: 6-quart

Prep: 13 minutes
Cook: 10 hours
Other: 8 hours

Leftover Ham Fixin's

Freeze leftover ham and ham bones until ready to use in this flavorful soup.

Quick Menu

- Spinach and fruit salad
- Biscuits

Chicken-and-Wild Rice Soup

2   tablespoons butter
3   celery ribs, thinly sliced
1   medium onion, chopped
1   (8-ounce) package sliced fresh baby
      portobello mushrooms
2   teaspoons minced garlic
4   (14-ounce) cans roasted garlic-flavored
      chicken broth (we tested with Swanson)
3   (6-ounce) packages roasted chicken breast
      chunks (we tested with Louis Rich)
1½ cups frozen whole kernel corn, thawed
      and drained
1   (8-ounce) can sliced water chestnuts,
      drained
1   cup uncooked wild rice
1   teaspoon salt
¾   teaspoon freshly ground pepper
2   cups whipping cream
Garnish: toasted slivered almonds

● Melt butter in a large skillet over medium-high heat.
Add celery and onion; cook 4 minutes or until almost
tender. Add mushrooms and garlic; cook 2 minutes.
● Combine mushroom mixture, broth, and next 6
ingredients in a 5-quart slow cooker.
● Cover and cook on LOW 5 to 6 hours or until rice
is tender. Stir in whipping cream. Garnish, if desired.
Makes 12½ cups.

Slow-Cooker Size: 5-quart

Prep: 12 minutes
Cook: 6 hours

Test Kitchen Secret

Roasted garlic-flavored
chicken broth is the secret
to fantastic flavor in this
soup. If you have a hard
time finding it, just ask
your grocer to order some
for you. If it is unavailable,
double the minced garlic.

Quick Menu

• Mixed greens salad with
cranberry or raspberry
vinaigrette
• Crusty French rolls

Chicken-Tortilla Soup

2 skinned and boned chicken breasts, cubed
1 (10-ounce) package frozen whole kernel corn, thawed
1 large onion, chopped
2 garlic cloves, pressed
2 (14-ounce) cans chicken broth
1 (10¾-ounce) can tomato puree
1 (10-ounce) can diced tomatoes and green chiles
¾ teaspoon salt
2 teaspoons ground cumin
1 teaspoon chili powder
⅛ teaspoon ground red pepper
⅛ teaspoon ground black pepper
1 bay leaf
4 (5½-inch) corn tortillas
Garnish: chopped fresh cilantro

- Combine first 13 ingredients in a 4-quart slow cooker.
- Cover and cook on HIGH 6 hours. Remove and discard bay leaf.
- Cut tortillas into ¼-inch-wide strips; place on a lightly greased baking sheet. Bake at 375° for 5 minutes. Stir strips, and bake 5 more minutes or until crisp. Serve with soup; garnish, if desired. Makes 10 cups.

Ham-and-White Bean Stew

2   (8-ounce) packages diced cooked ham
        (4 cups)
3   slices precooked bacon, chopped
1   small Vidalia onion, diced (about 1 cup)
1   (1-pound) bag baby carrots
2   celery ribs, chopped (about 1 cup)
2   (19-ounce) cans cannellini beans or
        navy beans, drained and divided
1   (14-ounce) can chicken broth
1   tablespoon chopped fresh or dried
        rosemary
1½ teaspoons chopped fresh thyme or
        ½ teaspoon dried thyme
½   teaspoon freshly ground black pepper

- Combine first 5 ingredients in a 4- or 5-quart slow cooker. Mash 1 can cannellini beans with a fork in a small bowl. Add mashed beans and remaining can beans to slow cooker. Stir in chicken broth and remaining ingredients.
- Cover and cook on HIGH 1 hour.
- Reduce heat to LOW, and cook 4 to 5 hours. Makes 9 cups.

Slow-Cooker Size: 4- or 5-quart

Prep: 15 minutes
Cook: 6 hours

Freeze It!
Freeze leftovers in single-serving containers up to 1 month.

Mashing one can of beans helps thicken this comforting stew.

Sweet Potato Stew with Red Beans

Slow-Cooker Size: 5-quart

Prep: 22 minutes
Cook: 7 hours

Beans 101

Red beans are different from kidney beans. They are smaller and rounder, like pinto beans, but red in color.

2   (10-ounce) cans diced tomatoes and mild green chiles (we tested with Rotel Mild)
1   (16-ounce) can red beans, rinsed and drained (we tested with Bush's)
1   (14-ounce) can vegetable broth
4   cups cubed peeled sweet potato (about 1½ pounds)
1   medium onion, chopped
1   small red bell pepper, chopped
½   cup water
1   garlic clove, minced
1   teaspoon grated fresh ginger
½   teaspoon salt
½   teaspoon ground cumin
¼   teaspoon black pepper
3   tablespoons creamy peanut butter
Chopped dry-roasted peanuts
Lime wedges (optional)

● Combine first 12 ingredients in a 5-quart slow cooker.
● Cover and cook on LOW 7 hours or until vegetables are tender.
● Spoon ½ cup cooking liquid into a small bowl. Add peanut butter to liquid, and stir well with a wire whisk. Stir peanut butter mixture into stew. Sprinkle each serving with peanuts. Serve with lime wedges, if desired. Makes 8 cups.

A squeeze of lime juice brightens the
rich, earthy flavors.

Texas Stew

2 pounds beef tips, cut into 1-inch cubes
1 (14½-ounce) can Mexican-style stewed
    tomatoes, undrained
1 (10½-ounce) can condensed beef broth,
    undiluted
1 (8-ounce) jar mild picante sauce
1 (10-ounce) package frozen whole kernel
    corn, thawed
3 carrots, cut into ½-inch pieces
1 onion, cut into thin wedges
2 garlic cloves, pressed
½ teaspoon ground cumin
½ teaspoon salt
½ cup water
¼ cup all-purpose flour

- Combine first 10 ingredients in a 5-quart slow cooker.
- Cover and cook on HIGH 3 to 4 hours or until meat is tender.
- Stir together ½ cup water and flour. Stir into meat mixture; cover and cook on HIGH 1 more hour or until thickened. Makes 12 cups.

Slow-Cooker Size: 5-quart

Prep: 10 minutes
Cook: 5 hours

Make Mine Spicy

Is mild picante sauce not spicy enough for you? Kick it up a notch with hot picante sauce. If you like it *really* hot, add chopped jalapeño.

Comfort Food • Editor's Favorite

Beef Burgundy Stew

This classic recipe, also known as Beef Bourguignonne, is slow-cooked with vegetables and red wine.

6	bacon slices, chopped
2	pounds beef stew meat
1	(16-ounce) package frozen pearl onions, thawed
1	(8-ounce) package fresh mushrooms, quartered
6	small red potatoes, quartered
2	large carrots, cut into ½-inch pieces
1	(14-ounce) can beef broth
1	cup Burgundy or dry red wine or beef broth
2	tablespoons tomato paste
1	tablespoon fresh thyme leaves
1	teaspoon salt
¼	teaspoon freshly ground black pepper
3	garlic cloves, minced
2	tablespoons cornstarch
2	teaspoons cold water

● Cook bacon in a large skillet over medium-high heat until crisp. Remove bacon, reserving drippings in pan. Set bacon aside.
● Brown beef, in batches, in reserved bacon drippings until browned on all sides.
● Combine reserved bacon, beef, onions, and next 10 ingredients in a 5-quart slow cooker. Cover and cook on LOW 7 hours or until beef and vegetables are tender.
● Whisk together cornstarch and water. Stir into stew. Cover and cook on HIGH 1 hour or until slightly thickened. Makes 9 cups.

Slow-Cooker Size: 5-quart

Prep: 17 minutes
Cook: 8 hours

Know Your Wine

We found that Burgundy best enhanced the flavor of this stew. If you don't have any on hand, any other dry red wine will do.

A hearty Burgundy is nice to sip with a bowl of stew laced with the same wine.

Chicken Brunswick Stew

2	large onions, chopped
6	skinned and boned chicken breasts
2	(14¾-ounce) cans cream-style corn
1	(28-ounce) can crushed tomatoes
1	(12-ounce) bottle chili sauce
1	(14-ounce) can chicken broth
¼	cup Worcestershire sauce
¼	cup butter or margarine, cut up
2	tablespoons cider vinegar
2	teaspoons dry mustard
½	teaspoon salt
½	teaspoon pepper
½	teaspoon pepper sauce

• Place onion in a 4-quart slow cooker; place chicken over onion. Add corn and remaining ingredients.

• Cover and cook on HIGH 4 hours or until chicken is tender. Remove chicken; shred and return to stew. Makes 14 cups.

Slow-Cooker Size: 4-quart

Prep: 10 minutes
Cook: 4 hours

Freeze It!

Store leftovers in zip-top freezer bags or freezer containers for quick weeknight meals.

Here's a great dinner soup or **side dish** for Southern-style barbecue.

15 Minutes or Less to Prep

Peasant Stew

1   teaspoon ground cumin
¼   teaspoon salt
¼   teaspoon black pepper
6   chicken thighs (about 2 pounds), skinned
1   cup chopped onion
1   (14½-ounce) can Mexican-style stewed
      tomatoes, undrained
1   (4.5-ounce) can chopped green chiles,
      undrained
1   (15-ounce) can pinto beans, rinsed and
      drained
1   (15-ounce) can kidney beans, rinsed and
      drained
¼   cup sour cream
¼   cup minced fresh cilantro

- Combine cumin, salt, and pepper; sprinkle over chicken.
- Place chicken in a 4- or 5-quart slow cooker; add onion, tomatoes, and chiles.
- Cover and cook on HIGH 3 hours. Stir in pinto and kidney beans.
- Cover and cook on HIGH 1 more hour.
- Top each serving with a dollop of sour cream, and sprinkle with cilantro. Makes 10 cups.

Slow-Cooker Size: 4- or 5-quart

Prep: 5 minutes
Cook: 4 hours

Serving Suggestion

Rice or rustic bread are ideal accompaniments for this stew.

The slight spice
of this stew is tamed
with sour cream.

Camp Stew

Slow-Cooker Size: 6-quart

Prep: 15 minutes
Cook: 8 hours

Substitution Ideas

Do you have a favorite barbecue joint? Feel free to substitute 10 ounces fresh cooked pork from your barbecue hot spot in place of the the 10-ounce can called for in the recipe.

1   pound ground beef
1   medium onion, chopped
2   large potatoes, peeled and diced
1   (16-ounce) package frozen speckled butter beans, thawed
1   (14¾-ounce) can creamed corn
1   (8¾-ounce) can whole kernel corn, drained
1   (10-ounce) can barbecued pork (we tested with Castleberry's Barbecue Pork)
1   (10-ounce) can white chicken in water, drained
2   (14½-ounce) cans stewed tomatoes
1   cup ketchup
1   cup water
2   to 4 tablespoons lemon juice
1   tablespoon Worcestershire sauce
1   teaspoon hot sauce
1   teaspoon salt
1   teaspoon pepper

● Cook ground beef and onion in a large skillet over medium-high heat, stirring until beef crumbles and is no longer pink; drain.
● Layer potato, butter beans, beef mixture, creamed corn, and remaining ingredients in a 6-quart slow cooker.
● Cover and cook on LOW 8 hours or until potato is tender. Makes 18 cups.

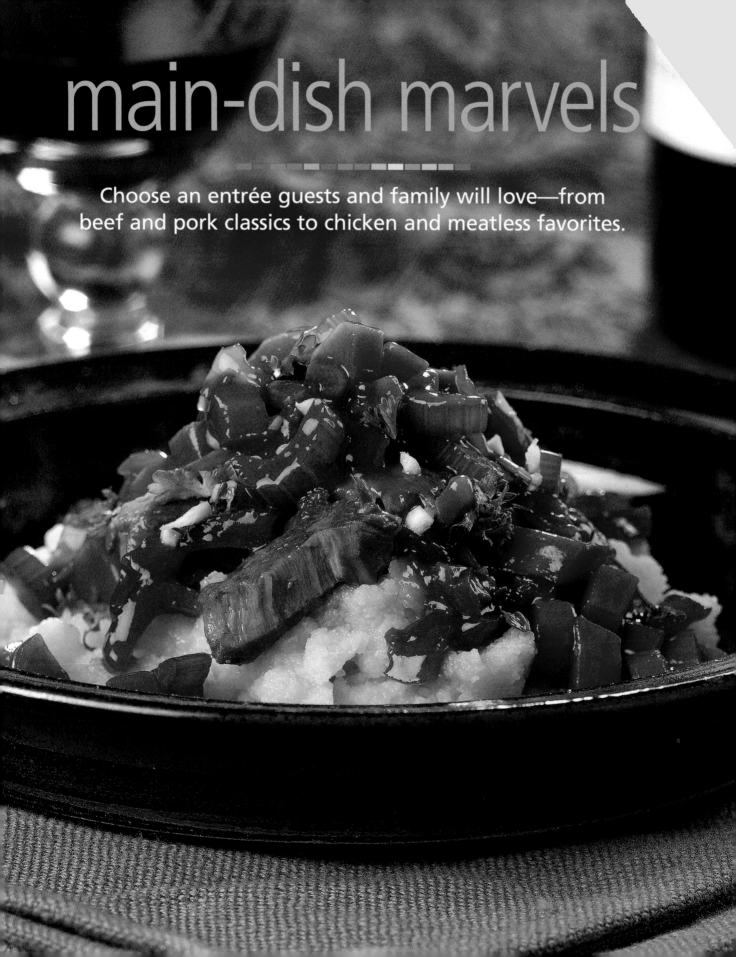

main-dish marvels

Choose an entrée guests and family will love—from beef and pork classics to chicken and meatless favorites.

Spicy Marinated Eye of Round

1   (3- to 5-pound) eye of round roast
½   teaspoon salt
¼   teaspoon pepper
3   sweet onions, sliced
Spicy Sauce
Garnish: chopped fresh parsley

● Cut roast in half, and sprinkle with salt and pepper. Place roast and onion in a 5-quart slow cooker. Stir together ingredients for Spicy Sauce, and pour mixture over uncooked roast.
● Cover and cook on HIGH 9 hours.
● Remove roast; cool slightly, and cut into thin slices. Return slices to sauce in slow cooker.
● Cover and cook on HIGH 1 more hour Garnish, if desired. Makes 8 to 10 servings.

Spicy Sauce

2   cups ketchup
2   cups water
2   large sweet onions, sliced
⅓   cup red wine vinegar
¼   cup firmly packed brown sugar
2   tablespoons Worcestershire sauce
1   teaspoon dry mustard
1   teaspoon dried oregano
1   teaspoon pepper
½   teaspoon garlic powder
½   teaspoon chili powder
½   teaspoon ground cloves
¼   teaspoon ground nutmeg
¼   teaspoon hot sauce
1   bay leaf

● Combine all ingredients. Makes 7 cups.

Barbecue Beef Sandwiches

1	(3½-pound) eye of round roast
2	teaspoons salt, divided
2	garlic cloves, pressed
1	(10½-ounce) can condensed beef broth, undiluted
1	cup ketchup
½	cup firmly packed brown sugar
½	cup lemon juice
3	tablespoons steak sauce
1	teaspoon coarse ground pepper
1	teaspoon Worcestershire sauce
12	Kaiser rolls or sandwich buns
	Dill pickle slices

● Cut roast in half, and sprinkle beef evenly with 1 teaspoon salt.

● Stir together remaining 1 teaspoon salt, garlic, and next 7 ingredients. Pour half of mixture into a 5½-quart slow cooker. Place beef in slow cooker, and pour remaining mixture over beef.

● Cover and cook on HIGH 7 hours.

● Shred beef in slow cooker with 2 forks. Serve on rolls with dill pickle slices. Makes 12 servings.

Slow-Cooker Size: 5½-quart

Prep: 15 minutes
Cook: 7 hours

Freeze It!

Freeze any leftover meat for up to 1 month.

Dual Slow-Cooker Menu

• Barbecue Baked Beans (page 152)
• Coleslaw

Set up a second slow cooker for Barbecue Baked Beans to simmer alongside the beef.

Mary's Roast Beef

Slow-Cooker Size: 4½-quart

Prep: 20 minutes
Cook: 7 hours, 5 minutes

Dual Slow-Cooker Menu
• Spinach-Artichoke Casserole (page 165)
• Baked potatoes

1   (3-pound) beef sirloin tip roast, cut in half
2   tablespoons vegetable oil
1   medium onion, chopped
2   garlic cloves, minced
1   cup brewed coffee
¾   cup water, divided
1   beef bouillon cube
1   teaspoon salt
2   teaspoons dried basil
½   teaspoon coarsely ground pepper
All-purpose flour
Garnish: fresh oregano sprig

● Brown all sides of roast on medium-high heat in hot oil in a large skillet 5 minutes on each side. Place roast in a 4½-quart slow cooker.

● Add onion and garlic to skillet, and sauté 2 minutes or until tender. Stir in 1 cup coffee, ½ cup water, bouillon cube, and next 3 ingredients until blended. Transfer to slow cooker.

● Cover and cook on LOW 6 to 7 hours or until tender. Transfer roast to a serving platter; measure drippings, and return to slow cooker. For every cup of drippings, add 1 tablespoon flour to the remaining ¼ cup water. Whisk to blend flour and water. Whisk mixture into drippings. Cook, uncovered, on HIGH 5 minutes or until gravy thickens, whisking frequently. Serve gravy with roast. Garnish, if desired. Makes 6 to 8 servings.

Easy Burritos

1   large onion, sliced into rings
1   (3- to 4-pound) sirloin beef roast, cut in half
½   cup water
2   (1.25-ounce) packages taco seasoning mix, divided
16 (6-inch) flour tortillas
4   cups (16 ounces) shredded Cheddar or Monterey Jack cheese
Toppings: diced tomatoes, diced onions, sliced jalapeño peppers, sour cream, black beans
Pico de Gallo

● Place onion in a 5-quart slow cooker; add roast and ½ cup water. Sprinkle 1 package taco seasoning mix over top of roast.
● Cover and cook on HIGH 5 hours. Remove roast, and shred with 2 forks; return to slow cooker, and stir in remaining package taco seasoning mix. Cover and cook on HIGH 30 more minutes.
● Heat tortillas according to package directions. Using a slotted spoon, spoon beef mixture evenly down centers of tortillas; top evenly with cheese and desired toppings, and roll up. Serve with Pico de Gallo. Makes 8 to 10 servings.

Pico de Gallo

3   cups diced plum tomatoes
½   cup diced red onion
⅓   cup chopped fresh cilantro
¼   to ⅓ cup diced jalapeño peppers
⅓   cup fresh lime juice
½   teaspoon olive oil
¼   teaspoon salt
¼   teaspoon black pepper

● Stir together all ingredients in a medium bowl. Cover and chill until ready to serve. Makes 3 cups.

Company's Coming

Italian Pot Roast

1   (8-ounce) package sliced fresh
      mushrooms
1   large onion, cut in half and sliced
1   (2½- to 3-pound) boneless chuck roast,
      trimmed
1   teaspoon pepper
2   tablespoons olive oil
1   (1-ounce) envelope dry onion soup mix
1   (14-ounce) can beef broth
1   (8-ounce) can tomato sauce
1   teaspoon dried Italian seasoning
3   tablespoons tomato paste
2   tablespoons cornstarch
2   tablespoons water
Toasted Herb Rice (page 169) or hot cooked
      egg noodles

- Place mushrooms and onion in a 5½-quart slow cooker.
- Sprinkle roast evenly with pepper. Brown roast on all sides in hot oil in a large Dutch oven over medium-high heat. Place roast on top of mushrooms and onion in slow cooker. Sprinkle onion soup mix evenly over roast. Pour beef broth and tomato sauce over roast.
- Cover and cook on HIGH 5 to 6 hours or until meat shreds easily with a fork.
- Remove roast from slow cooker, and cut into large chunks; keep warm.
- Skim fat from juices in slow cooker; stir in dried Italian seasoning and tomato paste. Stir together cornstarch and 2 tablespoons water in a small bowl until smooth; add to juices in slow cooker, stirring until blended.
- Cover and cook on HIGH 20 to 30 more minutes or until mixture is thickened. Add roast pieces back to slow cooker. Cover and cook until thoroughly heated. Serve over rice or noodles. Makes 6 servings.

Slow-Cooker Size: 5½-quart

Prep: 15 minutes
Cook: 6 hours, 40 minutes

Meat Substitution Tip

Chuck roast is one of the most economical cuts of beef for pot roast, but it is a high-fat choice. Substitute eye of round or English shoulder roast for a lower fat selection. You may need to cook it a little longer to get it tender.

Dual Slow-Cooker Menu

- Toasted Herb Rice (page 169) or buttered egg noodles
- Roasted asparagus

Beef Brisket with Fall Vegetables

2	(2-pound) beef briskets, trimmed
2	teaspoons salt
1	teaspoon pepper
1	tablespoon vegetable oil
4	carrots, peeled and cut into 2-inch pieces
3	parsnips, peeled and sliced
2	celery ribs, sliced
1	large onion, sliced
1	fennel bulb, quartered
12	fresh thyme sprigs
1	(1-ounce) envelope dry onion soup mix
1	(14-ounce) can low-sodium beef broth
¾	cup dry red wine
½	cup ketchup
2	tablespoons Beau Monde seasoning
8	garlic cloves
¾	cup chopped fresh parsley

Garnish: fresh thyme sprigs

- Sprinkle beef with salt and pepper.
- Heat oil over medium-high heat in a large nonstick skillet. Add beef; cook 4 minutes on each side or until browned. Transfer beef to a 6-quart slow cooker. Add carrot and next 5 ingredients.
- Whisk together soup mix and next 6 ingredients. Pour mixture evenly over beef.
- Cover and cook on LOW 12 hours or until tender. Transfer beef to a serving platter. Pour remaining vegetable mixture through a wire-mesh strainer, reserving juices, carrot, and onion; discard remaining vegetable mixture. Serve beef and vegetables with juices. Garnish, if desired. Makes 8 servings.

Slow-Cooker Size: 6-quart

Prep: 18 minutes
Cook: 12 hours

Quick Menu
- Roasted Garlic-Parmesan Mashed Potatoes (page 256)
- Bakery rolls

Corned Beef and Cabbage

1   (4-pound) cured corned beef brisket
        with spice packet
1   large onion, sliced
8   large carrots, halved lengthwise and cut
        into 2-inch pieces
2   bay leaves
3   garlic cloves, sliced
1   (14-ounce) can beef broth
2   tablespoons dark brown sugar
1½ tablespoons prepared mustard
1   teaspoon caraway seeds
1   small cabbage, cut into 8 wedges

• Trim fat from brisket. Place onion and carrot in a
6-quart slow cooker; place brisket on top of vegetables.
Sprinkle bay leaves and garlic slices over brisket.
• Combine spice packet from brisket, beef broth, sugar,
mustard, and caraway seeds; pour over brisket.
• Cover and cook on HIGH 1 hour. Reduce heat to LOW,
and cook 8 hours. Add cabbage, and cook on LOW 1½
hours or until cabbage is tender. Remove and discard bay
leaves and onion.
• Cut brisket across grain into slices; serve with cabbage
and carrots. Makes 6 to 8 servings.

Slow-Cooker Size: 6-quart

Prep: 16 minutes
Cook: 10 hours, 30 minutes

Quick Menu
• Pumpernickel rolls
• Dark beer

Sink your
teeth into this
tender classic.

Slow-Cooker Fajitas

Slow-Cooker Size: 5-quart

Prep: 12 minutes
Cook: 5 hours or 7 hours

Know Your Steak

Flank steak can be a tough cut of meat. Cooking in a slow cooker gives it fall-apart texture.

Dual Slow-Cooker Menu

• Peppered Corn on the Cob (page 155)
• Mexican beer

1½ pounds flank steak, cut into 4 to 6 pieces
1   medium onion, chopped
1   green bell pepper, sliced
1   jalapeño pepper, seeded and chopped
2   garlic cloves, pressed
1   tablespoon chopped fresh cilantro
1   teaspoon chili powder
1   teaspoon ground cumin
1   teaspoon ground coriander
¾   to 1 teaspoon salt
1   (10-ounce) can diced tomatoes and green chiles, drained
Flour tortillas
Toppings: shredded Cheddar cheese, sour cream, salsa
Garnish: cilantro sprigs

• Place steak in a 5-quart slow cooker; top with onion and next 9 ingredients.
• Cover and cook on HIGH 4 to 5 hours or on LOW 7 hours. Remove meat, and shred with 2 forks. Serve with tortillas and desired toppings. Garnish, if desired. Makes 4 to 6 servings.

Mexican spices in
these fajitas impart true
south-of-the-border
flavors.

Spaghetti Casserole

Slow-Cooker Size: 5-quart

Prep: 26 minutes
Cook: 4 hours
Other: 10 minutes

Kids Can Do It!

Get the kids involved in the preparation of this casserole. Let them break the spaghetti noodles or sprinkle the cheese in the slow cooker for a hands-on experience.

Quick Menu

• Caesar salad
• Garlic toast

1½ pounds ground round
1   medium onion, chopped
1   (26-ounce) jar tomato and basil pasta sauce
¼   cup butter
¼   cup all-purpose flour
1   (12-ounce) can evaporated milk
½   cup grated Parmesan cheese
¼   teaspoon pepper
8   ounces uncooked spaghetti, broken into pieces
3   cups (12 ounces) shredded sharp Cheddar cheese
Grated Parmesan cheese

• Cook ground round and onion in a large skillet, stirring until beef crumbles and is no longer pink; drain meat, and return to skillet. Stir pasta sauce into beef mixture.

• Melt butter in a saucepan over medium-low heat; whisk in flour until smooth. Cook 1 minute, whisking constantly. Gradually whisk in milk; cook over medium heat, whisking constantly, 8 minutes or until mixture is thickened and bubbly. Remove from heat, and stir in ½ cup Parmesan cheese and pepper.

• Spoon one-third of meat mixture into a lightly greased 5-quart slow cooker. Spread half of broken spaghetti over meat; pour half of white sauce over noodles, and sprinkle with 1 cup Cheddar cheese. Repeat layers once. Spread remaining meat mixture over cheese. Top with remaining 1 cup Cheddar cheese.

• Cover and cook on LOW 4 hours. Let stand 10 minutes before serving. Serve with Parmesan cheese. Makes 6 to 8 servings.

Creamy Beef and Spinach over Noodles

1   pound ground chuck
1   medium onion, chopped
1   (8-ounce) package sliced fresh
      mushrooms
1   (10-ounce) package frozen chopped
      spinach, thawed
1   (14-ounce) can low-sodium, fat-free beef
      broth
1   (10¾-ounce) can cream of mushroom
      soup
1   (8-ounce) container sour cream
½   teaspoon salt
¼   teaspoon pepper
1   (8-ounce) block Monterey Jack cheese
      with peppers, shredded
Hot cooked egg noodles

● Cook first 3 ingredients in a large skillet over medium heat, stirring until beef crumbles and is no longer pink; drain.
● Drain spinach well, pressing between paper towels. Combine beef mixture, spinach, broth, and next 5 ingredients in a large bowl. Spoon into a lightly greased 4-quart slow cooker. Cover and cook on LOW 4 hours. Serve over egg noodles. Makes 4 to 6 servings.

Slow-Cooker Size: 4-quart

Prep: 9 minutes
Cook: 4 hours

Quick Menu
• Fresh fruit salad
• Yeast rolls

Kelley's Famous Meat Loaf

1½ pounds ground round
1   (1-ounce) envelope dry onion soup mix
1   cup ketchup, divided
¼   cup water
¾   cup fine, dry breadcrumbs
1   large egg
1   cup (4 ounces) shredded sharp Cheddar
      cheese
1   tablespoon Worcestershire sauce
¼   teaspoon pepper
1   tablespoon light brown sugar
1   teaspoon prepared mustard

● Combine ground round, soup mix, ½ cup ketchup, and next 6 ingredients; shape mixture into an 8- x 4-inch loaf. Place loaf in a lightly greased 3-quart oval slow cooker.
● Cover and cook on HIGH 1 hour. Reduce heat to LOW, and cook 3 hours. Remove ceramic insert from cooker, and carefully pour grease off meat loaf; return insert to cooker.
● Stir together remaining ½ cup ketchup, brown sugar, and mustard in a small bowl; spread over meat loaf.
● Cover and cook on LOW 1 more hour or until meat loaf registers 160°. Remove meat loaf from ceramic insert, and let stand 10 minutes before serving. Makes 6 to 8 servings.

Slow-Cooker Size: 3-quart oval

Prep: 9 minutes
Cook: 5 hours
Other: 10 minutes

Leftover Fixin's

This comfort food is sure to please the whole family. Make sandwiches with leftovers the next day.

Quick Menu

• Refrigerated mashed potatoes
• Green beans

Meat loaf in the
slow cooker? You bet!
Using ground round
is the secret.

Open-Faced Meatball Sandwiches

These sandwiches are so versatile that they even please the pickiest eater at the dinner table. Just add your favorite pasta sauce and cheese to the meatball mixture, and serve over sesame, sourdough, white, or whole wheat hoagies.

Slow-Cooker Size: 3-quart

Prep: 5 minutes
Cook: 6 hours

Meatball Matters

This recipe can double as an appetizer without the bread—just have some toothpicks on hand, and serve the meatballs straight from the cooker.

24 frozen cooked Italian-style meatballs, thawed (we tested with Mama Mia)
1 (26-ounce) jar super chunky mushroom pasta sauce (we tested with Ragu Chunky Garden)
1 (15-ounce) can Italian-style tomato sauce (we tested with Hunt's Family Favorites)
1 (5.5-ounce) can spicy tomato juice (we tested with V8)
6 (6-inch) hoagie rolls, split but not cut through and toasted
1½ cups (6 ounces) shredded mozzarella cheese

● Combine first 4 ingredients in a 3-quart slow cooker.
● Cover and cook on HIGH 1 hour. Reduce heat to LOW, and cook 4½ to 5 hours or until slightly thickened. Spoon meatball mixture evenly into rolls. Sprinkle with cheese. Makes 6 servings.

Stuffed Cabbage Leaves

Slow-Cooker Size: 6-quart

Prep: 25 minutes
Cook: 5 hours

Cabbage Count

You may need to purchase 2 heads of cabbage so you can get 10 large whole cabbage leaves.

10 large cabbage leaves
¾ cup frozen diced onion, thawed
½ pound ground beef
½ pound ground pork
1 cup cooked long-grain rice
1 (14½-ounce) can diced tomatoes, drained
1 tablespoon olive oil
2 teaspoons salt
1 teaspoon pepper
1 teaspoon dried oregano
1 (32-ounce) jar sauerkraut, drained and divided
3½ cups spicy-hot vegetable juice, divided
2 tablespoons lemon juice

• Cook cabbage in boiling water to cover 3 minutes or just until pliable; drain. Set aside.
• Stir together onion and next 8 ingredients. Spoon about ⅓ cup meat mixture in center of each cabbage leaf; fold sides over meat mixture, and roll up.
• Place 2 cups sauerkraut in a 6-quart slow cooker. Pour 2 cups vegetable juice over sauerkraut. Top with cabbage rolls.
• Spoon remaining sauerkraut over cabbage rolls, and drizzle with remaining 1½ cups vegetable juice and lemon juice.
• Cover and cook on HIGH 1 hour. Reduce heat to LOW, and cook 4 hours or until done. Makes 5 servings.

Sauerkraut and Sausage

1   (32-ounce) jar sauerkraut
3   large garlic cloves, pressed
1   onion, chopped
1   large Granny Smith apple, peeled and
        coarsely chopped
¾   cup apple cider
2   tablespoons dark brown sugar
1   tablespoon white vinegar
1   teaspoon caraway seeds
½   teaspoon salt
½   teaspoon freshly ground pepper
1   (14-ounce) package smoked beef
        sausage, cut into 2-inch pieces
        (we tested with Hillshire Farms)

- Combine first 10 ingredients in a 3-quart slow cooker. Add sausage.
- Cover and cook on LOW 7 hours. Makes 4 servings.

Slow-Cooker Size: 3-quart

Prep: 9 minutes
Cook: 7 hours

Spicy!

If you'd like to add some heat to this German classic, use spicy sausage instead of regular.

Beef sausage adds a **little twist to the traditional** German family favorite made with ring bologna.

Osso Bucco with Gremolata

Made from parsley, garlic, and lemon rind, gremolata is used as a garnish to add fresh flavor to rich dishes.

2   tablespoons olive oil, divided
3   celery ribs, chopped (about 1 cup)
2   carrots, chopped (about 1 cup)
1   onion, chopped (about 1½ cups)
4   large garlic cloves, pressed
½   cup all-purpose flour
¾   teaspoon salt, divided
½   teaspoon pepper
4   (1½-inch-thick) veal shanks (about 3 pounds)
½   cup dry red wine
1   (14½-ounce) can diced tomatoes
1   (10½-ounce) can beef consommé
2   teaspoons fresh rosemary
1   teaspoon chopped fresh thyme
1   bay leaf
¼   cup chopped flat-leaf parsley
2   large garlic cloves, pressed
1   teaspoon grated lemon rind
4   cups cooked polenta

Slow-Cooker Size: 6-quart

Prep: 35 minutes
Cook: 9 hours

Quick Polenta

Making polenta doesn't always have to be time-consuming. Make it quickly using instant polenta, located in the pasta and rice section of your local supermarket.

● Heat 1 tablespoon oil in a large nonstick skillet over medium-high heat. Add celery and next 3 ingredients; sauté 3 minutes or until tender. Transfer vegetables to a 6-quart slow cooker.

● Combine flour, ½ teaspoon salt, and pepper in a large shallow dish. Dredge veal shanks in flour mixture.

● Heat remaining 1 tablespoon oil in skillet. Add veal shanks; cook 3 to 4 minutes on each side or until browned. Place shanks on top of vegetables in slow cooker. Add wine, next 5 ingredients, and remaining ¼ teaspoon salt to slow cooker; cover and cook on LOW 9 hours or until tender (meat should fall off bone). Remove veal shanks from slow cooker. Keep warm. Remove and discard bay leaf.

● Transfer vegetable mixture to a large saucepan. Bring mixture to a boil; reduce heat, and simmer 15 minutes or until slightly thickened. Meanwhile, combine parsley, garlic, and lemon rind. Serve veal and sauce over polenta. Sprinkle evenly with parsley mixture. Makes 4 servings.

Lamb Tagine

Slow-Cooker Size: 3- or 4-quart

Prep: 10 minutes
Cook: 4 hours, 5 minutes or
      7 hours, 5 minutes

Moroccan Flair

A *tagine* is a Moroccan dish slow-cooked with meat, fruit, and vegetables.

1½ pounds boneless leg of lamb, trimmed
    and cubed
2   tablespoons honey
½   teaspoon ground cinnamon
½   to ¾ teaspoon pepper
¼   teaspoon salt
¼   teaspoon ground ginger
¼   teaspoon saffron threads, crushed
1   (10½-ounce) can beef consommé
1½ cups frozen pearl onions, thawed and
    drained
½   cup bite-size dried pitted prunes, halved
2   tablespoons all-purpose flour
2   tablespoons water
Hot cooked couscous
¼   cup sesame seeds, toasted

• Place a nonstick skillet over medium-high heat until hot. Add lamb; sauté 5 minutes or until browned. Drain lamb, and place in a 3- or 4-quart slow cooker; stir in honey and next 6 ingredients.
• Cover and cook on HIGH 3 hours or on LOW 6 hours. Add onions and prunes. Cover and cook 1 more hour.
• Combine flour and water in a bowl; stir with a whisk until blended. Add to slow cooker.
• Cover and cook on HIGH 5 minutes or until thickened. Serve over couscous; sprinkle with sesame seeds. Makes 4 servings.

Rich flavors of
honey, cinnamon, and
saffron take you
to another world.

Creamy Lamb Curry

2½ pounds boneless leg of lamb, trimmed
  and cut into 1½-inch pieces
3 tablespoons vegetable oil, divided
1 cup small onion, chopped
2 garlic cloves, minced
1 tablespoon minced fresh ginger
2 bay leaves
1 (1-inch) cinnamon stick
1 teaspoon salt
2 teaspoons curry powder
2 teaspoons ground coriander
1 teaspoon ground cumin
½ teaspoon ground turmeric
⅛ teaspoon ground allspice
1 (13.5-ounce) can coconut milk
1 (14½-ounce) can diced tomatoes, undrained
½ cup plain yogurt
2 tablespoons chopped fresh mint
Hot cooked basmati rice
Toppings: chopped peanuts, raisins, toasted
  coconut, sliced green onions

● Brown half of lamb in 1 tablespoon hot oil in a large nonstick skillet over medium-high heat. Place cooked lamb in a 4-quart slow cooker. Brown remaining half of lamb in 1 more tablespoon hot oil; add to slow cooker.

● Add remaining 1 tablespoon oil to skillet; sauté onion, garlic, and ginger in hot oil 5 minutes or until tender. Add onion mixture to slow cooker. Add bay leaves and next 9 ingredients to slow cooker, stirring well.

● Cover and cook on HIGH 1 hour. Reduce heat to LOW, and cook 5 hours. Remove and discard bay leaves and cinnamon stick. Stir in yogurt and mint. Serve over hot cooked rice with desired toppings. Makes 6 servings.

Slow-Cooker Size: 4-quart

Prep: 30 minutes
Cook: 6 hours

Test Kitchen Secret

You can buy lamb stew meat, but a lamb roast you cut yourself will be leaner and more flavorful.

Quick Menu

• Basmati rice
• Raita (yogurt and fruit salad)
• Indian flat bread

Thai-Style Ribs

3½ pounds pork baby back ribs, racks cut
    in half
1   (11.5-ounce) can frozen orange-
    pineapple-apple juice concentrate,
    thawed and undiluted (we tested with
    Welch's)
¾   cup soy sauce
¼   cup creamy peanut butter
¼   cup minced fresh cilantro
2   tablespoons minced fresh ginger
1   garlic clove, pressed
2   teaspoons sugar
Garnish: fresh cilantro sprigs

- Place ribs in a large shallow dish or zip-top freezer bag.
- Combine juice concentrate and next 6 ingredients in a small bowl with a wire whisk. Reserve ¾ cup mixture in refrigerator for dipping. Pour remaining mixture evenly over ribs; cover or seal, and chill 8 hours, turning occasionally.
- Remove ribs from marinade, discarding marinade. Place 1 rack of ribs in bottom of a 6-quart slow cooker; stand remaining rib racks on their sides around edges of slow cooker. Cover and cook on HIGH 1 hour. Reduce heat to LOW, and cook 5 hours.
- Microwave reserved ¾ cup sauce in a 1-cup glass measure at HIGH 1 to 1½ minutes or until thoroughly heated, stirring once. Serve with ribs. Garnish, if desired. Makes 2 to 4 servings.

Slow-Cooker Size: 6-quart

Prep: 10 minutes
Cook: 6 hours
Other: 8 hours

Stand Your Ribs

Standing these ribs along the sides of your slow cooker gives them direct contact with heat, so they'll have crispy brown edges like ribs that have smoked for hours.

These ribs marinate all night and then slow-cook all day to get their incredible flavor.

Spicy-Sweet Ribs and Beans

Slow-Cooker Size: 5-quart

Prep: 30 minutes
Cook: 6 hours or 10 hours
Other: 20 minutes

Flavor Tip

Slow cookers don't brown food, so here we broil the ribs for extra flavor before adding them to the pot.

Quick Menu

• Green salad with creamy Italian or Ranch-style dressing
• Cornbread

2   (16-ounce) cans pinto beans, drained
4   pounds country-style pork ribs, trimmed
1   teaspoon garlic powder
½   teaspoon salt
½   teaspoon pepper
1   medium onion, chopped
1   (10.5-ounce) jar red jalapeño pepper jelly
1   (18-ounce) bottle hickory-flavored barbecue sauce (we tested with Kraft Thick 'n Spicy)
1   teaspoon green hot sauce (we tested with Tabasco)

• Place beans in a 5-quart slow cooker; set aside.
• Cut ribs apart; sprinkle with garlic powder, salt, and pepper. Place ribs on a broiling pan. Broil 5½ inches from heat 18 to 20 minutes or until browned, turning once. Add ribs to slow cooker, and sprinkle with onion.
• Combine jelly, barbecue sauce, and hot sauce in a saucepan; cook over low heat until jelly melts. Pour over ribs; stir gently.
• Cover and cook on HIGH 5 to 6 hours or on LOW 9 to 10 hours. Remove ribs. Drain bean mixture, reserving sauce. Skim fat from sauce. Arrange ribs over bean mixture; serve with sauce. Makes 8 servings.

Saucy Barbecue Ribs

4 pounds country-style pork ribs, trimmed
2 teaspoons salt, divided
1 medium onion, chopped
1 cup firmly packed light brown sugar
1 cup apple butter
1 cup ketchup
½ cup lemon juice
½ cup orange juice
1 tablespoon steak sauce (we tested with A1)
1 teaspoon coarse ground pepper
1 teaspoon minced garlic
½ teaspoon Worcestershire sauce

- Cut ribs apart; sprinkle 1 teaspoon salt evenly over ribs, and set aside.
- Stir together remaining 1 teaspoon salt, chopped onion, and remaining 9 ingredients until blended. Pour half of mixture into a 5- or 6-quart slow cooker. Place ribs in slow cooker; pour remaining mixture over ribs.
- Cover and cook on HIGH 6 to 7 hours. Makes 6 to 8 servings.

Slow-Cooker Size: 5- or 6-quart

Prep: 15 minutes
Cook: 7 hours

Make-Ahead Tip

Put these ribs on to cook before you leave for work, or cook them overnight and refrigerate until dinnertime. If you reheat in the microwave, use 50% power.

Dual Slow-Cooker Menu

- Peppered Corn on the Cob (page 155)
- Texas toast

Serve this with Texas toast
for soppin' up
the sauce.

Country Pork and Corn on the Cob

Slow-Cooker Size: 4½-quart

Prep: 14 minutes
Cook: 4 hours

Substitution Tip

Substitute frozen ears of corn when fresh corn is out of season.

½ cup all-purpose flour
1½ teaspoons salt, divided
1   teaspoon pepper, divided
6   (5-ounce) bone-in center-cut pork chops
      (about ½-inch-thick)
2   to 3 tablespoons olive oil, divided
4   large garlic cloves, pressed
3   ears fresh corn, cut in half
1   (18-ounce) bottle honey smoke barbecue
      sauce (we tested with KC Masterpiece)
1   cup chicken broth

• Combine flour, 1 teaspoon salt, and ½ teaspoon pepper in a large zip-top freezer bag; add pork, tossing to coat.
• Heat 1 tablespoon oil in a large nonstick skillet over medium-high heat. Cook pork, in 2 batches, 2 minutes on each side or until browned, adding additional 1 tablespoon oil if needed.
• Place in a lightly greased 4½-quart slow cooker. Rub remaining 1 tablespoon oil and garlic evenly over corn. Sprinkle with remaining ½ teaspoon each salt and pepper; add to slow cooker. Combine barbecue sauce and broth; add to slow cooker.
• Cover and cook on LOW 4 hours or until meat is tender. Makes 6 servings.

Using your favorite bottled barbecue sauce allows you to make this rustic farm dish in just a few easy steps.

Apple Cider Pork and Vegetables

4   small sweet potatoes, peeled and cut
      into ½-inch slices
1   (6-ounce) package dried mixed fruit
1   medium onion, thinly sliced
1   bay leaf
¾   teaspoon salt
½   teaspoon pepper
½   teaspoon dried rosemary, crushed
1½ pounds lean boneless pork, cut into
      1-inch pieces
½   cup all-purpose flour
2   tablespoons vegetable oil
1   cup apple cider

- Place first 7 ingredients in a 5-quart slow cooker.
- Dredge pork in flour; brown in hot oil in a skillet over medium-high heat. Remove pork, reserving drippings in skillet. Place pork in cooker. Stir apple cider into reserved drippings; pour over pork.
- Cover and cook on LOW 6 to 8 hours or until pork and sweet potatoes are tender. Remove and discard bay leaf. Makes 4 servings.

Slow-Cooker Size: 5-quart

Prep: 15 minutes
Cook: 8 hours

Quick Menu
- Buttered broccoli spears
- Raisin bread toast

Saucy Chipotle Barbecue Pork

2   teaspoons dry mustard
1   teaspoon salt
½   teaspoon ground red pepper
1   (4- to 5-pound) boneless pork butt roast,
       cut in half
2   tablespoons butter
1   large onion, chopped (about 2½ cups)
1   (18-ounce) bottle spicy original barbecue
       sauce (we tested with KC Masterpiece)
1   (12-ounce) bottle Baja chipotle marinade
       (we tested with Lawry's)
Garnish: sliced green onions

- Rub first 3 ingredients evenly over pork. Melt butter in a large nonstick skillet over medium-high heat. Add pork; cook 10 minutes or until browned on all sides.
- Place onion and pork in a 5-quart slow cooker. Add barbecue sauce and marinade.
- Cover and cook on HIGH 7 hours or until pork is tender and shreds easily.
- Remove pork to a large bowl, reserving sauce; shred pork. Stir shredded pork into sauce. Serve as is, over a cheese-topped baked potato, in a sandwich, or over a green salad. Garnish, if desired. Makes 8 servings.

Slow-Cooker Size: 5-quart

Prep: 15 minutes
Cook: 7 hours

Saucy Solutions

This spicy barbecue pork recipe cooks up an ample amount of sauce—a delicious bonus for barbecue sauce lovers. Use it for dripping over a sandwich, dipping fries, or dressing baked potatoes.

Spicy barbecue sauce and chipotle marinade mingle to make this barbecue **pack extra punch.**

Easy Spanish Pork Dip Sandwiches

Slow-Cooker Size: 6-quart

Prep: 20 minutes
Cook: 6 hours

Test Kitchen Secret

The secret ingredient in this recipe is the Spanish marinating sauce.

3 tablespoons garlic pepper
2 teaspoons salt
1 (4- to 5-pound) boneless pork butt roast, cut in half
¼ cup vegetable oil
¾ cup mojo criollo Spanish marinating sauce (we tested with La Lechonora Mojo Criollo)
2 (0.75-ounce) envelopes pork gravy mix
2 cups water
¼ cup white vinegar
2 bay leaves
1 medium-size sweet onion, thinly sliced
1 fresh Cuban bread loaf

• Sprinkle garlic pepper and salt evenly over roast. Cook roast in hot oil in a large skillet 2 minutes on each side or until lightly browned. Place in a 6-quart slow cooker, fat sides up.
• Combine Spanish marinating sauce and next 3 ingredients; pour over roast in slow cooker. Add bay leaves; top with sliced onion.
• Cover and cook on HIGH 1 hour. Reduce heat to LOW, and cook 4 to 5 hours or until meat is tender and shreds easily. Remove and discard bay leaves.
• Remove pork and onion to a large bowl, reserving liquid; shred pork. Add 1 cup reserved liquid to shredded pork to moisten.
• Slice bread into 8 equal portions; slice each portion in half lengthwise. Place shredded pork on bottom bread slices; top with remaining bread slices.
• Spoon remaining reserved liquid into individual bowls for dipping. Makes 8 sandwiches.

Sausage 'n' Tater Casserole

You can omit the ground red pepper for the "mild" members of your family.

- 1 (16-ounce) package hot ground pork sausage
- 1 onion, chopped (about 1 cup)
- 4 large garlic cloves, pressed
- 1 (10¾-ounce) can Southwest-style pepper Jack soup
- 1 (10¾-ounce) can cream of onion soup
- 1 (10¾-ounce) can Cheddar cheese soup
- ¼ teaspoon ground red pepper
- 1 (32-ounce) package frozen potato tots, partially thawed

● Cook first 3 ingredients in a large nonstick skillet, stirring until meat crumbles and is no longer pink. Stir in soups and pepper.

● Arrange half of potato tots in a lightly greased 5-quart slow cooker. Spread meat mixture evenly over potato tot layer. Arrange remaining potato tots evenly over meat layer.

● Cover and cook on HIGH 1 hour. Reduce heat to LOW, and cook 4½ hours or until edges are golden. Makes 6 servings.

Slow-Cooker Size: 5-quart

Prep: 12 minutes
Cook: 5 hours, 30 minutes

What a Surprise!

Even folks who don't care for potato tots enjoy this tasty concoction. Your whole family will gobble it up.

This is **comfort food** for the kid in all of us.

Spicy Sausage Grits

2 cups uncooked regular grits
2 (14-ounce) cans chicken broth
2 cups heavy whipping cream
1 (10¾-ounce) can Cheddar cheese soup
1 jalapeño pepper, minced
2 cups frozen whole kernel corn, thawed
1½ teaspoons salt
1½ teaspoons hot sauce
½ pound hot smoked sausage, sliced
      (we tested with Hillshire Farms)
3 tablespoons butter

● Combine first 8 ingredients in a 4-quart slow cooker. Stir in sausage.
● Cover and cook on LOW 4½ hours or until thickened, stirring once after 3 hours. Stir in butter, and serve immediately. Makes 6 servings.

Slow-Cooker Size: 4-quart

Prep: 10 minutes
Cook: 4 hours, 30 minutes

Sausage Substitution Tip

Use andouille sausage or regular smoked sausage if you find the hot smoked sausage too spicy.

With a spicy blend of sausage, corn, and creamy cheese grits, you can't go wrong serving this great version of a Southern classic to your non-Southern guests.

Creole Sausage with Rice and Beans

1   (16-ounce) package smoked sausage, sliced
2   (10-ounce) cans diced tomatoes with green chiles
3½ cups fat-free, less-sodium chicken broth
2   teaspoons Creole seasoning
1½ cups uncooked converted long-grain rice
2   (15-ounce) cans red beans, rinsed and drained

● Cook sausage in a large skillet over medium heat 5 minutes or until browned; drain. Place sausage in a 4-quart slow cooker; stir in tomatoes and next 3 ingredients.
● Cover and cook on LOW 3½ hours. Stir in beans. Cover and cook on HIGH 30 minutes or until thoroughly heated. Makes 8 servings.

Six simple ingredients pack lots of flavor in this hearty dish.

Roasted Chicken with Vegetables

Slow-Cooker Size: 5-quart

Prep: 17 minutes
Cook: 3 hours, 30 minutes
Other: 8 hours

Make-Ahead Tip

Bone and chop this chicken, and it's a tender and tasty make-ahead for other recipes that call for chopped cooked chicken.

3 quarts water
1 tablespoon salt
1 (3½- to 4-pound) whole chicken, cut in half
2 tablespoons butter, softened
2 tablespoons lemon pepper
2 carrots, coarsely chopped
2 celery ribs, coarsely chopped
1 medium onion, coarsely chopped
1 lemon, quartered
2 garlic cloves, halved
1 cup chicken broth

● Combine water and salt in a large bowl; add chicken. Cover and chill 8 hours.
● Drain chicken; rinse with cold water, and pat dry. Spread softened butter evenly over chicken skin. Sprinkle evenly with lemon pepper. Place chicken halves on a small wire rack in a 5-quart slow cooker. Arrange carrots and next 4 ingredients around chicken. Pour broth over all ingredients.
● Cover and cook on HIGH 3½ hours or until a thermometer inserted into thigh registers 180°. Makes 4 servings.

Brining (soaking in salty water) makes chicken extra juicy and tender.

Easy Chicken Cassoulet

8 skinned and boned chicken thighs
     (about 1¾ pounds)
3 tablespoons olive oil, divided
1 (8-ounce) package sliced fresh
     mushrooms
2 teaspoons minced fresh rosemary
½ cup vermouth
4 (16-ounce) cans navy beans, drained and
     rinsed
1 cup shredded Parmesan cheese
1 cup coarse soft French breadcrumbs,
     toasted and divided
½ teaspoon salt
½ teaspoon pepper
1 (12-ounce) jar mushroom gravy (we
     tested with Heinz Homestyle Rich
     Mushroom Gravy)

Slow-Cooker Size: 4-quart

Prep: 20 minutes
Cook: 6 hours

Test Kitchen Secret

A slow-cooker cassoulet tends to be thinner than a traditional cassoulet because the juices don't evaporate. Serve it with toasted French bread to enjoy all the robust juices.

● Brown chicken in 1 tablespoon hot oil in a large skillet over medium-high heat 5 minutes on each side. Remove chicken from skillet, and place in a 4-quart slow cooker.
● Add remaining 2 tablespoons oil to skillet. Add mushrooms and rosemary; sauté 3 minutes. Stir in vermouth, and cook 5 minutes. Spoon mushrooms over chicken. Add 2 cans navy beans to slow cooker. Sprinkle with ½ cup cheese, ½ cup breadcrumbs, salt, and pepper; drizzle with gravy. Add remaining 2 cans beans and remaining ½ cup Parmesan cheese.
● Cover and cook on HIGH 1 hour. Reduce heat to LOW, and cook 5 hours. Sprinkle with remaining breadcrumbs. Makes 4 to 6 servings.

Mu Shu Chicken Wraps

1   medium onion, diced
2   pounds skinned and boned chicken
      thighs
¼   teaspoon salt
¼   teaspoon pepper
1   tablespoon sesame or vegetable oil
¾   cup hoisin sauce
1   tablespoon soy sauce
1   tablespoon honey
2   teaspoons rice wine
¼   teaspoon ground ginger
8   (6-inch) flour tortillas
3   cups shredded napa cabbage
½   cup thinly sliced green onions

- Place onion in a 3- or 4-quart slow cooker.
- Sprinkle chicken evenly with salt and pepper.
- Brown chicken 2 to 3 minutes on each side in hot oil in a large skillet over medium-high heat. Remove skillet from heat, and place chicken on top of onion in slow cooker.
- Whisk together hoisin sauce and next 4 ingredients; pour over chicken. Cover and cook on HIGH 1 hour. Reduce heat to LOW, and cook 5 hours. Shred chicken in cooker with fork.
- Top each tortilla evenly with cabbage, chicken, and green onions. Fold bottom edge of each tortilla in to hold filling; roll tortilla crosswise, and, if desired, secure with wooden picks or parchment paper. Makes 8 servings.

Slow-Cooker Size: 3- or 4-quart

Prep: 11 minutes
Cook: 6 hours

Appetizer Option

Wrap the spicy chicken mixture in lettuce or cabbage leaves to serve as appetizers.

Package these tasty wraps in **parchment paper** for an upscale bistro experience.

Shredded Barbecue Chicken

Slow-Cooker Size: 4-quart

Prep: 22 minutes
Cook: 7 hours

Serving Suggestion

Spoon this saucy chicken over a crisp green salad or a baked potato instead of a bun, if you'd like.

1½ pounds skinned and boned chicken
    thighs
1   tablespoon olive oil
1   cup ketchup
¼   cup dark brown sugar
1   tablespoon Worcestershire sauce
1   tablespoon cider vinegar
1   tablespoon yellow mustard
1   teaspoon ground red pepper
½   teaspoon garlic salt
6   hamburger buns
Dill pickle slices

- Brown chicken 4 minutes on each side in 1 tablespoon hot oil in a large skillet over medium-high heat. Remove from heat, and place in a 4-quart slow cooker.
- Combine ketchup and next 6 ingredients. Pour over chicken.
- Cover and cook on HIGH 1 hour. Reduce heat to LOW, and cook 5 to 6 hours. Remove chicken from sauce; shred chicken. Stir shredded chicken into sauce. Spoon mixture evenly onto buns, and top with pickle slices. Makes 6 servings.

Serve with golden fries and a little bowl of ketchup **for dunking** the fries.

Loaded Jambalaya

Slow-Cooker Size: 5-quart

Prep: 25 minutes
Cook: 5 hours, 15 minutes

Lid Tip

If you prefer a thicker jambalaya, leave the lid off while cooking the shrimp during the last 15 minutes to concentrate the juices.

¾ pound skinned and boned chicken thighs, cut into 1-inch pieces
¾ pound skinned and boned chicken breasts, cut into 1-inch pieces
1 teaspoon salt
⅛ teaspoon black pepper
⅛ teaspoon ground red pepper
2 tablespoons vegetable oil
1 large onion, chopped (about 2 cups)
1 large green bell pepper, chopped
2 celery ribs, chopped
4 garlic cloves, minced
1 (14½-ounce) can diced tomatoes, undrained
½ pound fully cooked ham, cut into ½-inch pieces
1 (14-ounce) can chicken broth
2 (3.5-ounce) bags boil-in-bag rice
1 pound medium-size fresh shrimp
½ cup chopped green onions
2 tablespoons chopped fresh parsley
1 tablespoon hot sauce (we tested with Frank's Hot Sauce)

● Sprinkle chicken evenly with salt, black pepper, and red pepper.
● Heat oil in a large skillet over high heat. Add chicken; cook 4 to 5 minutes, stirring occasionally, or until browned. Spoon chicken into a 5-quart slow cooker.
● Add onion and next 3 ingredients to skillet; sauté 4 minutes or until tender. Transfer to slow cooker. Add tomatoes, ham, and broth to slow cooker.
● Cover and cook on LOW 5 hours. Meanwhile, cook rice according to package directions. Set aside.
● Peel shrimp, and devein, if desired. Stir shrimp, cooked rice, and remaining ingredients into slow cooker. Cover and cook on HIGH 15 minutes or until shrimp turn pink. Makes 4 to 6 servings.

Kids Love It!

Chicken-and-Wild Rice Hot Dish

4	skinned and boned chicken breasts (about 2 pounds)
1	cup chopped onion
1	cup chopped celery
5	garlic cloves, pressed
2	(6-ounce) packages uncooked long-grain and wild rice mix (we tested with Uncle Ben's)
2	(14-ounce) cans chicken broth with roasted garlic
2	(10¾-ounce) cans cream of mushroom soup
1	(8-ounce) package sliced fresh mushrooms
1	(8-ounce) can sliced water chestnuts, drained
1	cup chopped walnuts, toasted
2	tablespoons butter

- Brown chicken in a lightly greased large nonstick skillet over medium-high heat; remove from pan, and cut into ½-inch pieces. Add onion, celery, and garlic to pan; sauté 3 to 4 minutes or until tender.
- Combine rice mix and remaining 6 ingredients in a 5-quart slow cooker. Stir in chicken and vegetables.
- Cover and cook on LOW 4 hours or until rice is tender and liquid is absorbed. Makes 6 servings.

Slow-Cooker Size: 5-quart

Prep: 15 minutes
Cook: 4 hours

Quick Menu
- Steamed carrots
- Green salad

With an earthy blend of wild rice, mushrooms, and walnuts, this is a great casserole to serve the family on a cool autumn evening.

Buffalo Chicken Tender Salad

Slow-Cooker Size: 3-quart

Prep: 20 minutes
Cook: 3 hours

Saucy Matters

To enjoy the full flavor potential of this salad, we suggest a buffalo sauce that has a nice spice without overpowering heat.

1½ pounds chicken tenderloins
1¼ cups buffalo wing sauce (we tested with Moore's)
1   (10-ounce) package torn romaine lettuce
1   pint cherry tomatoes, cut in half
5   bacon slices, cooked and crumbled
¾   cup julienne carrot
½   cup sliced celery
2   ounces blue cheese, crumbled
1   cup refrigerated blue cheese dressing (we tested with Naturally Fresh)

● Combine chicken and buffalo wing sauce in a 3-quart slow cooker.
● Cover and cook on HIGH 3 hours.
● Combine lettuce and next 5 ingredients in a large bowl. Divide evenly among serving plates. Top with cooked chicken. Drizzle evenly with dressing. Makes 4 servings.

Here's the **nonmessy way** to enjoy the taste of buffalo chicken.

Chicken and Rice Casserole

1 (6.2-ounce) package fast cooking
    long-grain and wild rice mix
2 tablespoons butter
1 medium onion, chopped
2 celery ribs, chopped
3 cups chopped cooked chicken
3 cups (12 ounces) shredded colby-Jack
    cheese blend, divided
1 (10¾-ounce) can cream of mushroom
    soup
1 (8-ounce) container sour cream
½ cup milk
½ teaspoon salt
½ teaspoon pepper
1 cup crushed round buttery crackers

- Prepare rice mix according to package directions.
- Meanwhile, melt butter in a large skillet over medium-high heat; add onion and celery. Sauté 4 minutes or until tender.
- Combine rice, sautéed vegetables, chicken, 2 cups cheese, and next 5 ingredients; spoon into a lightly greased 5-quart slow cooker.
- Cover and cook on LOW 4½ hours. Combine remaining 1 cup cheese and cracker crumbs; sprinkle over casserole.
- Cover and cook on LOW 30 more minutes. Makes 6 servings.

Slow-Cooker Size: 5-quart

Prep: 18 minutes
Cook: 5 hours

Chicken Choices

Rather than cooking and chopping chicken, use the meat from a deli-roasted chicken. It will yield just enough for this recipe.

Quick Menu

- Spinach salad
- Soft breadsticks

Crunchy topping from a slow cooker? You bet—with this last-minute cracker trick!

Chicken Enchiladas

3   cups chopped cooked chicken
2   cups (8 ounces) shredded Monterey Jack
      cheese with peppers
1   (4.5-ounce) can chopped green chiles
½   cup sour cream
⅓   cup chopped fresh cilantro
8   (8-inch) flour tortillas
1   (8-ounce) container sour cream
1   (8-ounce) bottle green taco sauce
1   cup (4 ounces) shredded Monterey Jack
      cheese with peppers
Toppings: chopped tomato, chopped
      avocado, sliced green onions, sliced
      ripe olives, chopped fresh cilantro

● Stir together first 5 ingredients. Spoon chicken mixture evenly down center of tortillas, and roll up. Arrange, seam sides down, in a lightly greased 6-quart slow cooker, stacking tortillas, if needed.
● Stir together sour cream and taco sauce; spoon over enchiladas. Cover and cook on LOW 4½ hours. Remove lid, and sprinkle enchiladas with 1 cup cheese.
● Cover and cook on LOW 15 more minutes or until cheese melts. Serve with desired toppings. Makes 8 enchiladas.

Slow-Cooker Size: 6-quart

Prep: 18 minutes
Cook: 4 hours, 45 minutes

Quick Menu
• Refried beans
• Tortilla chips

Enchiladas are supereasy in the slow cooker. Melting cheese over the top at the last minute and adding colorful toppings dress them for company.

Chicken Burritos

2 cups chopped cooked chicken
1 (1.25-ounce) package taco seasoning mix
1 (16-ounce) can refried beans
8 (8-inch) flour tortillas
1 (8-ounce) package shredded sharp
    Cheddar cheese
3 plum tomatoes, chopped
½ cup minced onion
Salsa verde

● Place chicken and seasoning mix in a large zip-top freezer bag; seal and shake to coat chicken.
● Spread beans evenly over tortillas. Top each with chicken, cheese, tomato, and onion; roll up. Wrap each burrito in aluminum foil; place in a 5- or 6-quart slow cooker.
● Cover and cook on HIGH 2 hours. Serve with salsa verde. Makes 8 burritos.

Slow-Cooker Size: 5- or 6-quart

Prep: 20 minutes
Cook: 2 hours

Salsa Sub

Any type of salsa can be substituted for salsa verde, which is a green salsa made from tomatillos.

Quick Menu

• Spanish rice
• Fresh honeydew wedges

Burritos steam in individual foil packets for easy serving and **sealed-in flavor.**

Chicken Lasagna Florentine

1   (10-ounce) package frozen chopped
      spinach, thawed
2   cups chopped roasted chicken
1   (10¾-ounce) can cream of chicken and
      mushroom soup, undiluted
1   (10¾-ounce) can cream of onion soup,
      undiluted
1   (8-ounce) container sour cream
1   cup milk
1   (8-ounce) package sliced fresh
      mushrooms, chopped
½   teaspoon pepper
¼   teaspoon salt
3½ cups (14 ounces) shredded colby-Jack
      cheese blend, divided
9   uncooked lasagna noodles
1   cup freshly shredded Parmesan cheese
½   cup chopped pecans

● Drain spinach well, pressing between paper towels to
remove excess moisture.
● Stir together spinach, chicken, and next 7 ingredients in
a large bowl; stir in 2 cups colby-Jack cheese.
● Arrange 3 uncooked noodles in a lightly greased 5-quart
slow cooker, breaking noodles as necessary to fit in slow
cooker. Spread one-third of chicken mixture over noodles;
sprinkle with ½ cup colby-Jack cheese. Repeat layers twice.
Sprinkle with Parmesan cheese and pecans.
● Cover and cook on LOW 3½ to 4 hours or until noodles
are done. Let stand 10 minutes before serving. Makes 6 to
8 servings.

Slow-Cooker Size: 5-quart

Prep: 25 minutes
Cook: 4 hours
Other: 10 minutes

Shortcut

Use any cooked chicken
you have on hand—we
prefer using a rotisserie
chicken because it's
extra tasty.

Indulge in this cheesy
no-fuss lasagna recipe
that layers uncooked noodles.

Creole Chicken and Okra with Red Beans

4	cups shredded deli-roasted chicken
3	cups frozen cut okra, thawed
2	(10-ounce) bags frozen seasoning blend, thawed
2	(16-ounce) cans red beans, drained
1	(14½-ounce) can diced tomatoes
1	jalapeño pepper, minced
2	garlic cloves, minced
1½	teaspoons Creole seasoning
2	teaspoons hot sauce

● Combine first 8 ingredients in a 5- or 6-quart slow cooker.

● Cover and cook on LOW 5 hours. Stir in hot sauce before serving. Makes 8 servings.

Slow-Cooker Size: 5- or 6-quart

Prep: 17 minutes
Cook: 5 hours

Test Kitchen Secret

A typical rotisserie chicken yields 3 to 4 cups chopped cooked chicken. Buy a chicken on the large side, at least 2½ pounds, to make sure to get the 4 cups needed for this recipe.

Serve this dish over white or brown rice for a warming one-dish dinner. Pass extra hot sauce for added spice.

Comfort Food

Sausage-and-White Bean Cassoulet

2   (16-ounce) cans great Northern beans, undrained
1   (28-ounce) can diced tomatoes, undrained
1   (14-ounce) package smoked turkey sausage, sliced
¾   cup vegetable broth
3   medium carrots, sliced
1   cup frozen chopped onion, thawed
2   garlic cloves, minced
½   teaspoon salt
½   teaspoon dried thyme
¼   teaspoon pepper
1   bay leaf
½   cup fine, dry breadcrumbs
¼   cup freshly grated Parmesan cheese

- Combine first 11 ingredients in a 5-quart slow cooker.
- Cover and cook on LOW 8 hours or until vegetables are tender. Remove and discard bay leaf.
- Stir in breadcrumbs. Sprinkle each serving with Parmesan cheese before serving. Makes 6 servings.

Slow-Cooker Size: 5-quart

Prep: 10 minutes
Cook: 8 hours

Quick Menu
- Tossed green salad
- Vinaigrette

Comfort Food • Kids Love It!

Cheesy Chicken Casserole

4   cups shredded cooked chicken
1   (10¾-ounce) can chicken and mushroom
    soup
1   (8-ounce) container sour cream
¼   teaspoon pepper
1   (8-ounce) block sharp Cheddar cheese,
    shredded and divided
25 round buttery crackers, coarsely crushed

● Stir together first 4 ingredients and 1½ cups cheese; spoon into a lightly greased 3-quart slow cooker. Cover and cook on LOW 3 hours.
● Combine remaining cheese and cracker crumbs; sprinkle over casserole. Cover and cook on LOW 1 more hour. Let stand 5 minutes before serving. Makes 4 to 6 servings.

This simple casserole
pleases even
the pickiest eater.

Spanish-Style Lentils and Rice

1 cup dried lentils
1 cup uncooked long-grain rice (we tested
      with Uncle Ben's)
1 medium onion, chopped
1 medium-size green bell pepper, chopped
2 (14-ounce) cans chicken broth
1 (10-ounce) can diced tomatoes and
      green chiles
1 teaspoon salt
1 teaspoon chili powder
½ teaspoon ground cumin
¼ teaspoon garlic powder
1½ cups (6 ounces) shredded sharp Cheddar
      cheese

● Place lentils in a 4-quart slow cooker. Cover with
water 2 inches above lentils; let soak 8 hours. Drain and
rinse; return lentils to slow cooker. Add rice and next 8
ingredients.
● Cover and cook on LOW 4 hours or until lentils and rice
are tender. Stir in cheese and serve immediately. Makes
6 to 8 servings.

Slow-Cooker Size: 4-quart

Prep: 8 minutes
Cook: 4 hours
Other: 8 hours

Serving Tip

This dish starts to thicken
as it sets. For best consistency and flavor, serve
immediately.

This **protein-packed** dish is 100 percent comfort food in every sense. With Cheddar cheese and spicy diced tomatoes, it makes for a well-rounded meal.

Polenta-and-Mushroom Alfredo Lasagna

Slow-Cooker Size: 6-quart

Prep: 22 minutes
Cook: 4 hours
Other: 15 minutes

Saucy Matters

You'll fool guests into thinking you've spent hours in the kitchen making your own Alfredo sauce when you use jarred sauce in this classy dish.

Quick Menu

- Grilled Italian sausage
- Caesar salad

2	(3.5-ounce) packages fresh shiitake mushrooms
1	(8-ounce) package sliced fresh mushrooms
1	medium onion, cut in half crosswise and sliced vertically
3	tablespoons olive oil
2	(16-ounce) jars Alfredo sauce (we tested with Classico)
¼	cup dry white wine
½	teaspoon freshly ground pepper
¼	teaspoon ground nutmeg
2	(17-ounce) tubes pesto-flavored or plain polenta, cut into ½-inch slices (we tested with Marjon Basil and Garlic Polenta)
1	cup freshly grated Parmesan cheese

• Remove and discard stems from shiitake mushrooms; thinly slice mushrooms. Sauté mushrooms and onion in hot oil in a large skillet over medium-high heat until onion is tender and liquid is absorbed.

• Whisk together Alfredo sauce, wine, pepper, and nutmeg; stir into mushroom mixture. Spread 3 tablespoons mushroom mixture in a 6-quart slow cooker. Layer one-third of polenta slices over sauce. Sprinkle ½ cup Parmesan cheese over polenta; top with half of remaining mushroom mixture. Layer one-third of polenta slices and remaining half of mushroom mixture; top with remaining one-third of polenta slices. Sprinkle with remaining ½ cup Parmesan cheese.

• Cover and cook on LOW 4 hours or until set. Remove lid, and let lasagna stand 15 minutes before serving. Makes 6 servings.

This recipe is **versatile** enough to be a main dish or a side dish.

slow-cooked sides

Rounding out a meal is easy with these
veggie, pasta, and rice choices.

Barbecue Baked Beans

This recipe's 12-hour cook time allows you the flexibility to go to work, come home, fire up the grill, and entertain guests—the beans will be done just in time for dinner to be served.

1   (20-ounce) package dried Cajun 15-bean soup mix (we tested with Hurst's HamBeens brand)
1   (12-ounce) package diced cooked ham (we tested with Hormel)
2   cups chicken broth
1   cup chopped onion
1   (18-ounce) bottle hickory smoke barbecue sauce (we tested with KC Masterpiece)
¼   cup firmly packed light brown sugar
¼   cup molasses
½   teaspoon salt
¼   teaspoon ground red pepper

● Reserve spice packet in soup mix for other uses. Place beans in a large glass bowl; add water 2 inches above beans. Microwave at HIGH 15 minutes; cover and let stand 1 hour. Drain.
● Combine beans, ham, broth, and onion in a 4-quart slow cooker. Combine barbecue sauce and remaining 4 ingredients; stir into bean mixture.
● Cover and cook on LOW 12 hours or until beans are tender and sauce is slightly thickened. Makes 9 servings.

Slow-Cooker Size: 4-quart

Prep: 20 minutes
Cook: 12 hours
Other: 1 hour

Test Kitchen Secret

The tenderness of beans varies depending on the age and type of the beans. Each package may cook differently.

Barbecue chicken or ribs to accompany these tangy-sweet beans.

Creamy Ranch Cauliflower

If cauliflower is a "forgotten" vegetable in your home, this recipe is sure to bring it back to your dinner table.

1   (15.25-ounce) can Mexican-style corn, drained
1   (10¾-ounce) can cream of onion soup
1   (8-ounce) container sour cream
1   (8-ounce) container chive-and-onion cream cheese, softened
1   (1-ounce) envelope Ranch-style dressing mix
1   jalapeño pepper, minced
3   (10-ounce) packages fresh cauliflower florets
3   bacon slices, cooked and crumbled (optional)

- Combine first 6 ingredients in a 4-quart slow cooker. Add cauliflower, stirring well to coat.
- Cover and cook on LOW 5½ to 6 hours or until tender. Sprinkle with bacon, if desired. Makes 6 servings.

Slow-Cooker Size: 4-quart

Prep: 10 minutes
Cook: 6 hours

Fresh Florets

Cauliflower florets are available both fresh and frozen in 10-ounce packages, but be sure to use the fresh packages from the produce department—you'll have better results.

Ranch-style dressing makes cauliflower **rich and creamy.**

Peppered Corn on the Cob

6   tablespoons butter, softened
4   garlic cloves, pressed
6   ears fresh corn, husks removed
1   teaspoon freshly ground black pepper
½   teaspoon salt
12   fully cooked bacon slices (we tested with
       Ready Crisp Bacon)
½   cup chicken broth
1   jalapeño pepper, minced

● Combine butter and garlic in a small bowl. Rub garlic butter evenly over ears of corn. Sprinkle evenly with pepper and salt. Wrap each ear of corn with 2 bacon slices, and secure with wooden picks. Place corn in a 5-quart slow cooker. Add broth and jalapeño pepper.
● Cover and cook on LOW 3 to 4 hours or until corn is tender. Remove bacon before serving, if desired. Makes 6 servings.

Slow-Cooker Size: 5-quart

Prep: 13 minutes
Cook: 4 hours

Bacon Bit

If you don't want to wrap the bacon around the corn, simply chop the bacon and sprinkle on top of the corn in the cooker.

Bacon imparts a **smoky flavor** that makes this corn dish like no other.

Editor's Favorite • Southern Classic

Slow-Cooked Collard Greens

1	smoked turkey wing (about 1¼ pounds)
2	(14-ounce) cans Italian-seasoned chicken broth
2	(1-pound) packages chopped fresh collard greens
5	green onions, chopped
1	green bell pepper, seeded and coarsely chopped
¾	teaspoon salt
½	teaspoon black pepper
	Pepper sauce

● Remove skin and meat from turkey wing, discarding skin and bone. Coarsely chop meat.
● Combine chopped turkey and next 6 ingredients in a 6-quart slow cooker.
● Cover and cook on LOW 9 hours or until greens are tender. Serve with pepper sauce. Makes 10 to 12 servings.

Slow-Cooker Size: 6-quart

Prep: 5 minutes
Cook: 9 hours

Soppin' Up

Have some corn bread or rolls handy for sopping up the juices.

Dual Slow-Cooker Menu

● Ready-to-bake macaroni and cheese
● Hot-and-Spicy Black-Eyed Peas (page 161)
● Deli cornbread

A sprinkling of pepper sauce is the ultimate **Southern condiment** for these greens.

Myra's Burgundy Mushrooms

3   pounds fresh button mushrooms
1½ cups Burgundy or other dry red wine
1   (14-ounce) can beef broth
½   cup butter, cut into pieces
1   tablespoon Worcestershire sauce
1   teaspoon salt
½   teaspoon garlic powder
½   teaspoon dried dillweed
½   teaspoon pepper

● Place mushrooms in a 6-quart slow cooker. Add Burgundy and remaining ingredients to slow cooker.
● Cover and cook on LOW 10 hours. Serve with a slotted spoon. Makes 8 servings.

There'll be
no last-minute
tending to the
mushroom side dish with
this slow-cooker technique.

Slow-Cooker Size: 6-quart

Prep: 15 minutes
Cook: 10 hours

Leftover Delight

The delicious juices left over after cooking the mushrooms can be used for a multitude of other dishes. Try thickening 1½ cups liquid with 1½ table-spoons all-purpose flour for a tasty sauce with French dip sandwiches. You can also pour the juices into ice cube trays, freeze, and pop out later to flavor soups or vegetables.

Quick Menu
• Grilled filet mignon
• Baked potatoes

Caramelized Onions

2 bacon slices
2 tablespoons butter, melted
2 medium-size sweet onions, sliced
    (about 4½ cups)
¼ teaspoon salt
⅛ teaspoon pepper

• Cook bacon in a skillet until crisp; remove bacon, reserving 1 tablespoon drippings. Reserve bacon for another use.
• Combine drippings, melted butter, and remaining ingredients in a 3- or 4-quart slow cooker. Stir well to coat onions.
• Cover and cook on HIGH 4 hours. Makes 2 cups.

French Onion Soup: Stir 2 (10½-ounce) cans beef consommé and ¼ cup dry white wine into cooked onions in slow cooker. Cover and cook on HIGH 15 minutes or just until heated. Sprinkle with shredded Gruyère cheese and restaurant-style croutons. Makes 5 cups.

Slow-Cooker Size: 3- or 4-quart

Prep: 10 minutes
Cook: 4 hours

Serving Suggestion

These savory onions are great served as a side dish for grilled steak or chicken, piled on a roast beef sandwich, or used as a pizza topping.

This French Onion Soup variation received our Test Kitchen's highest rating.

Big Batch

Hot-and-Spicy Black-Eyed Peas

- 1 (16-ounce) package dried black-eyed peas
- 4 green onions, chopped
- 1 red bell pepper, chopped
- 1 jalapeño pepper, diced
- 1 (3-ounce) package pepperoni slices, diced
- 2 cups hot water
- 1 chicken bouillon cube
- ½ teaspoon salt
- ¼ teaspoon ground red pepper
- 1 (14½-ounce) can Mexican-style stewed tomatoes
- ¾ cup uncooked quick rice

Slow-Cooker Size: 5-quart

Prep: 20 minutes
Cook: 8 hours, 30 minutes
Other: 8 hours

Quick Menu
- Deli coleslaw
- Cornbread

- Place peas in a 5-quart slow cooker. Cover with water 2 inches above peas; let stand 8 hours. Drain.
- Combine peas and next 8 ingredients in slow cooker.
- Cover and cook on LOW 8 hours or until beans are tender. Stir in tomatoes and rice. Cover and cook on LOW 30 more minutes or until rice is tender. Makes 12 cups.

Jalapeño pepper and Mexican-style stewed tomatoes spice up these black-eyed peas.

Mexican Spoonbread-Stuffed Poblanos

Poblano chile peppers range in heat. They are usually mild but can sometimes be surprisingly spicy.

6	poblano chile peppers
¾	cup self-rising cornmeal mix (we tested with Martha White)
⅔	cup chopped frozen onion, thawed
1	(8-ounce) can cream-style corn
1	cup (4 ounces) shredded colby-Jack cheese
1	large egg, lightly beaten
¼	cup milk
2	tablespoons butter or margarine, melted
2	tablespoons canned chopped green chiles
½	teaspoon salt
⅛	teaspoon hot sauce

● Lay peppers on sides. Lengthwise slice off top quarter of peppers to create shells. Reserve removed portions of peppers for other uses. Scrape out seeds using a small spoon; discard seeds.

● Combine cornmeal mix and remaining 9 ingredients in a medium bowl. Spoon cornmeal mixture evenly into pepper shells. Arrange peppers in a 6-quart oval slow cooker. Cover and cook on HIGH 4 hours. Makes 6 servings.

Slow-Cooker Size: 6-quart oval

Prep: 20 minutes
Cook: 4 hours

Test Kitchen Secret

We used frozen chopped onion to make sure it was tender after cooking. If you use freshly chopped onion, cook it briefly in the microwave or finely chop it before cooking.

Southern Classic

Apple-Pecan Sweet Potatoes

Many sweet potato dishes taste very sweet because lots of sugar and sometimes marshmallows are added. This creamy version is subtly sweet with a hint of tart apple—perfect for those people who prefer to truly enjoy the taste of sweet potato.

4	large sweet potatoes, peeled and cut into 1½-inch cubes
1½	cups peeled and chopped Granny Smith apple (1 large apple)
1	cup chicken broth
½	cup whipping cream
¼	cup firmly packed light brown sugar
2	tablespoons butter
½	teaspoon salt
¾	teaspoon ground cinnamon
¾	cup chopped pecans, toasted

● Combine first 3 ingredients in a 5-quart slow cooker. Cover and cook on LOW 8 hours or until potatoes are tender; drain, discarding broth.
● Add whipping cream and next 4 ingredients; beat at medium speed with an electric mixer until smooth and blended. Stir in pecans. Makes 6 servings.

Slow-Cooker Size: 5-quart

Prep: 15 minutes
Cook: 8 hours

Quick Menu
• Honey-glazed ham
• Green beans

This simple side allows you to reserve the oven for the "Quick Menu" accompaniments.

Ratatouille

Slow-Cooker Size: 6-quart

Prep: 20 minutes
Cook: 8 hours

Serving Suggestion

Pair this dish with creamy polenta to turn this veggie side into a hearty meatless main dish.

1   large eggplant, peeled and cut into
     1-inch cubes (about 1½ pounds)
1   large onion, chopped
2   tomatoes, chopped
1   large green bell pepper, cut into
     ½-inch pieces
1   large red bell pepper, cut into
     ½-inch pieces
3   medium zucchini, chopped
3   garlic cloves, minced
3   tablespoons olive oil
1   tablespoon capers
1   teaspoon salt
½   teaspoon black pepper
¼   cup tomato paste
1   (4½-ounce) can sliced black olives,
     drained
¼   cup chopped fresh basil
½   cup grated Parmesan cheese

● Combine first 11 ingredients in a 6-quart slow cooker.
● Cover and cook on LOW 8 hours.
● Stir in tomato paste, olives, and basil. Sprinkle with Parmesan cheese. Makes 8 to 10 servings.

Spinach-Artichoke Casserole

1	tablespoon butter or margarine
1	(8-ounce) package sliced fresh mushrooms
2	garlic cloves, pressed
1	tablespoon lemon juice
½	teaspoon pepper
2	(10-ounce) packages frozen chopped spinach, thawed
1	(14-ounce) can quartered artichoke hearts, drained and chopped
1	(10¾-ounce) can reduced-fat, reduced-sodium cream of mushroom soup
1	(8-ounce) container reduced-fat sour cream
3	green onions, chopped
2	tablespoons all-purpose flour
1	tablespoon chopped fresh parsley
¼	teaspoon Worcestershire sauce
2	cups (8 ounces) shredded Monterey Jack cheese with peppers

Slow-Cooker Size: 4-quart

Prep: 20 minutes
Cook: 2 hours or 4 hours

Party Tip

Choose to serve this casserole as a side dish or as an appetizer. Toasted Melba rounds make sturdy dippers for serving this dish straight out of the pot.

• Melt butter in a large skillet over medium-high heat. Add mushrooms and next 3 ingredients; sauté 5 minutes.
• Meanwhile, drain spinach well, pressing between paper towels. Stir together spinach and next 7 ingredients.
• Stir mushroom mixture into spinach mixture. Add 1 cup cheese, stirring well. Spoon into a 4-quart slow cooker. Sprinkle with remaining 1 cup cheese.
• Cover and cook on HIGH 2 hours or on LOW 4 hours. Makes 8 to 10 servings.

Glazed Winter Vegetables

¼   cup butter or margarine, melted
¼   cup firmly packed brown sugar
¼   teaspoon ground nutmeg
½   teaspoon ground cinnamon
½   teaspoon pepper
4   medium parsnips, peeled and cut
       into ½-inch cubes
4   medium carrots, peeled and cut
       into ½-inch cubes
2   medium-size sweet potatoes, peeled and
       cut into ½-inch cubes
½   medium rutabaga, peeled and cut
       into ½-inch cubes

• Stir together first 5 ingredients in a 6-quart slow cooker;
add vegetables, tossing to coat.
• Cover and cook on LOW 6 to 7 hours or until vegetables
are tender. Makes 8 servings.

Mexican Macaroni

1   (8-ounce) package elbow macaroni,
    uncooked
1   (10-ounce) can diced tomatoes and
    green chiles, undrained
1   (10¾-ounce) can cream of mushroom
    soup, undiluted
1   cup water
1   (8-ounce) container sour cream
1   (4.5-ounce) can chopped green chiles
2   cups (8 ounces) shredded Mexican
    four-cheese blend

- Stir together first 6 ingredients in a bowl; stir in 1½ cups cheese. Pour mixture into a lightly greased 3-quart slow cooker; top with remaining ½ cup cheese.
- Cover and cook on LOW 4½ hours or until macaroni is done. Makes 6 servings.

Slow-Cooker Size: 3-quart

Prep: 7 minutes
Cook: 4 hours, 30 minutes

Spicy!

This dish is an interesting spin on the typical mac-and-cheese recipe. Green chiles give this dish just enough kick to make it spicy.

There's no need to precook the macaroni for this easy mac-and-cheese dish.

Toasted Herb Rice

3   tablespoons butter or margarine
1¾ cups uncooked converted long-grain rice
        (we tested with Uncle Ben's)
2   (14-ounce) cans chicken broth
¼   teaspoon salt
6   green onions, chopped
1   teaspoon dried basil
⅓   cup pine nuts, toasted
Garnish: fresh basil sprig

● Melt butter in a large skillet over medium-high heat; add rice, and sauté 4 minutes or until golden brown. Combine sautéed rice, broth, and next 3 ingredients in a 4-quart slow cooker.
● Cover and cook on HIGH 2 hours or until liquid is absorbed and rice is tender. Stir in pine nuts. Garnish, if desired. Makes 6 servings.

Slow-Cooker Size: 4-quart

Prep: 7 minutes
Cook: 2 hours

Fresh Is Best

If you have fresh basil on hand, use 1 tablespoon fresh instead of 1 teaspoon dried basil.

Toasted pine nuts dress up rice with a **pleasant crunch.**

Applesauce

12 large Granny Smith apples (about
      5½ pounds)
¼ cup fresh lemon juice
1½ cups sugar

• Peel, core, and cut apples into 1½-inch chunks. Place chunks in a large bowl. Toss apple with lemon juice and sugar. Place apple mixture in a 6-quart slow cooker.
• Cover and cook on HIGH 4 hours. Stir until desired consistency. Store in an airtight container in refrigerator up to 1 week. Makes 8 cups.

Slow-Cooker Size: 6-quart

Prep: 20 minutes
Cook: 4 hours

Pick an Apple

We like the tanginess of Granny Smith apples in this recipe. If you use sweeter apples, you may need to adjust the sugar and cook time.

These apples hold their shape well during cooking, so the sauce ends up chunky. Stir the sauce to smooth it to the consistency you like.

Fresh Mango Chutney

6   whole cloves
4   whole allspice
4   whole cardamom seeds
1   (3-inch) cinnamon stick, broken
1½ cups peeled, diced ripe mango
     (about 2 large)
¾   cup coarsely chopped onion
¾   cup cider vinegar
¾   cup firmly packed light brown sugar
¼   cup golden raisins
1½ teaspoons minced fresh ginger
1   jalapeño pepper, cut in half lengthwise
1   garlic clove, minced

- Place first 4 ingredients in a 4-inch square of cheese-cloth; tie with string.
- Combine mango and remaining 7 ingredients in a 3-quart slow cooker. Add spice bag.
- Cover and cook on HIGH 10 hours or until thickened. Remove and discard jalapeño pepper halves and spice bag. Stir chutney to blend flavors. Cool. Store in an airtight container in refrigerator up to 1 week. Makes 1⅔ cups.

Slow-Cooker Size: 3-quart

Prep: 15 minutes
Cook: 10 hours

Serving Suggestion

This sweet and spicy condiment complements a wide variety of meats. Serve it over a spice-rubbed pork, honey-glazed ham, minted lamb, or grilled chicken.

Tomato Relish

Serve over garlic-toasted baguette slices, pork, or your favorite cracker.

Slow-Cooker Size: 4-quart

Prep: 21 minutes
Cook: 10 hours

Homegrown

Making this relish is a great way to use tomatoes from your garden.

Dual Slow-Cooker Menu

• Grilled pork tenderloin
• Peppered Corn on the Cob (page 155)

4   large tomatoes, seeded and chopped
2   garlic cloves, minced
1   medium onion, finely chopped
3   tablespoons chopped fresh basil
2   tablespoons light brown sugar
2   tablespoons cider vinegar
1   tablespoon olive oil
1   teaspoon fennel seeds
½   teaspoon salt
¼   teaspoon pepper

● Combine all ingredients in a 4-quart slow cooker.
● Cover and cook on LOW 10 hours or until thickened and liquid is almost absorbed. Cool. Store in an airtight container in refrigerator up to 1 week. Serve with a slotted spoon. Makes 2¾ cups.

slow-cooked sweets

Create a sweet-tooth bonanza in your slow cooker
with delicious cakes, puddings, and candies.

Mocha Pudding Cake

1⅓ cups sugar
1   cup all-purpose flour
½   cup butter, melted
4   large eggs, lightly beaten
⅓   cup unsweetened cocoa
¼   cup chopped pecans, toasted
2   teaspoons instant coffee granules
½   teaspoon ground cinnamon
¼   teaspoon salt
2   teaspoons vanilla extract
Vanilla ice cream (optional)

● Stir together all ingredients except ice cream in a large bowl. Pour into a lightly greased 3-quart slow cooker.
● Cover and cook on LOW 2 to 2½ hours or until set around the edges but still soft in the center. Let stand, covered, 30 minutes. Serve warm with ice cream, if desired. Makes 6 to 8 servings.

Here's the ultimate rich and **fudgy** dessert—part cake and part pudding!

Cookie-Crusted Rhubarb-Cherry Dessert

Slow-Cooker Size: 4-quart

Prep: 5 minutes
Cook: 5 hours

Cookie Crunch

We used plain shortbread cookies, but you can use the variety with pecans if you'd like.

1½ cups firmly packed light brown sugar
⅓ cup all-purpose flour
2   (16-ounce) packages frozen cut rhubarb
2   (14.5-ounce) cans pitted tart cherries, drained
1   tablespoon lemon juice
1   tablespoon butter
2   teaspoons vanilla extract
2   cups coarsely chopped shortbread cookies

● Stir together sugar and flour in a 4-quart slow cooker. Add rhubarb, cherries, and lemon juice, tossing to coat.
● Cover and cook on LOW 5 hours. Stir in butter and vanilla. Sprinkle each serving with coarsely chopped cookies. Makes 8 servings.

This recipe gives a **cookie twist** to a traditional crisp.

Apple Crisp

8   large Granny Smith apples,
      peeled and sliced (about 4 pounds)
1½ cups all-purpose baking mix, divided
1   cup firmly packed light brown sugar,
      divided
2   teaspoons lemon juice
2   teaspoons vanilla extract
1   teaspoon ground cinnamon
¼   teaspoon ground nutmeg
5   tablespoons butter, cut into pieces and
      divided
Vanilla ice cream

● Combine apples, ½ cup baking mix, ½ cup brown sugar, lemon juice, and next 3 ingredients, tossing to coat. Add 3 tablespoons butter. Spoon into a lightly greased 5-quart slow cooker.

● Combine remaining 1 cup baking mix and remaining ½ cup brown sugar; cut in remaining 2 tablespoons butter with a pastry blender until crumbly. Sprinkle evenly over apple mixture.

● Cover and cook on LOW 7½ hours or until apples are tender and topping is golden. Serve with ice cream. Makes 6 servings.

Slow-Cooker Size: 5-quart

Prep: 30 minutes
Cook: 7 hours, 30 minutes

Apple Picker

The type of apples used in an apple crisp or pie can make or break the dessert. Use an all-purpose or cooking apple, such as Granny Smith, Fuji, Braeburn, or other hand-picked apples straight from your local orchard.

Peaches 'n' Cream Tapioca

4 cups fresh or frozen peach slices
     (about 2 pounds)
3 tablespoons uncooked quick-cooking
     tapioca
¾ cup firmly packed brown sugar
⅛ teaspoon salt
⅛ teaspoon ground nutmeg
1 cup heavy whipping cream
½ cup peach nectar
2 cups granola

- Stir together first 7 ingredients in a 3½-quart slow cooker.
- Cover and cook on LOW 4 hours. Stir well; spoon into dessert dishes, and top evenly with granola. Makes 8 servings.

Slow-Cooker Size: 3½-quart

Prep: 6 minutes
Cook: 4 hours

Peachy Keen
Fresh peaches are best. If you use frozen ones, just rinse off any ice crystals; there's no need to thaw them for this recipe.

Granola gives this homey dessert a **crunch** similar to a peach crisp.

Cinnamon-Raisin Bread Pudding

Slow-Cooker Size: round 6-quart

Prep: 13 minutes
Cook: 3 hours
Other: 1 hour

Test Kitchen Secret

To quickly make 1-inch bread cubes, stack bread slices and cut vertically into thirds; then cut cross-wise into thirds.

3   large eggs, beaten
½   cup sugar
1   teaspoon ground cinnamon
¼   teaspoon ground nutmeg
1   cup milk
1   cup whipping cream
1   teaspoon vanilla extract
2   tablespoons butter or margarine, melted
1   (1-pound) cinnamon-raisin bread loaf, cut into 1-inch cubes
½   cup chopped pecans, toasted
Whipped cream (optional)

• Whisk together first 4 ingredients in a large bowl; stir in milk, cream, vanilla, and butter. Add bread cubes and pecans, stirring gently just until bread is moistened. Cover and chill 1 hour.

• Pour bread mixture into a lightly greased 2½-quart soufflé dish; cover with aluminum foil. Pour 1 cup water into a 6-quart round slow cooker; place a wire rack to fit cooker on bottom. Set soufflé dish on rack.

• Cover and cook on HIGH 3 hours or until a sharp knife comes out clean. Cool slightly before serving. Serve warm with whipped cream, if desired. Makes 8 servings.

A slow cooker gives this classic dessert the gentle heat it needs to cook to perfection.

Caramel Bread Pudding

3   large eggs
2½ cups milk
1   cup whipping cream
¾   cup sugar
¼   teaspoon ground nutmeg
¼   teaspoon ground cinnamon
1   (12-ounce) day-old French bread loaf,
        cut into 1-inch cubes
½   cup raisins
1   (20-ounce) bottle caramel topping
        (we tested with Smucker's Caramel
        Sundae Syrup)

● Whisk together first 6 ingredients in a large bowl. Add bread cubes and raisins, stirring gently to blend. Cover and chill 1 hour.
● Spoon bread mixture into a lightly greased 5-quart slow cooker.
● Cover and cook on LOW 4½ hours or until set. Serve with caramel topping. Makes 6 to 8 servings.

Slow-Cooker Size: 5-quart

Prep: 10 minutes
Cook: 4 hours, 30 minutes
Other: 1 hour

On Hand

If you keep a bottle of caramel topping in the pantry, you can make this recipe any time you have leftover French bread.

Caramel topping turns this simple bread pudding into something extra special.

Maple-Glazed Pears

6   Bosc pears, peeled, cored, and halved
     (pears need to be firm but ripe)
½   cup firmly packed light brown sugar
2   tablespoons maple syrup
2   tablespoons butter or margarine,
     melted
⅛   teaspoon ground ginger
⅛   teaspoon ground cinnamon
Vanilla ice cream (optional)
Caramel sauce (optional)

• Place pears in a 4-quart slow cooker.
• Combine brown sugar and next 4 ingredients in a small bowl. Pour over pears.
• Cover and cook on LOW 4 hours or until pears are tender but still hold their shape. Serve warm plain or with ice cream and caramel sauce. Makes 6 servings.

Slow-Cooker Size: 4-quart

Prep: 13 minutes
Cook: 4 hours

Test Kitchen Secret

We found that Bosc pears worked best in this recipe. They tend to be drier and firmer than other varieties, which makes them perfect for the slow cooker.

Tender pears in a buttery brown sugar sauce beg for a scoop of ice cream— caramel sauce takes them over the top.

Comfort Food

Cinnamon Apples

6   medium Granny Smith apples, peeled
      and cut into eighths
1   tablespoon lemon juice
½   cup firmly packed dark brown sugar
½   cup chopped walnuts
½   cup maple syrup
¼   cup sweetened dried cranberries
      (we tested with Craisins)
¼   cup butter, melted
2   teaspoons ground cinnamon
2   tablespoons water
1   tablespoon cornstarch

- Combine apples and lemon juice in a 4-quart slow cooker; toss well to coat. Add brown sugar and next 5 ingredients, combining well.
- Cover and cook on LOW 3 hours.
- Stir together water and cornstarch in a small bowl; stir into apples.
- Cover and cook on LOW 3 more hours or until apples are tender. Makes 6 to 8 servings.

Slow-Cooker Size: 4-quart

Prep: 16 minutes
Cook: 6 hours

Serving Suggestion
Serve these sweet apples alone or over ice cream or pound cake.

The aroma of
cinnamon scents
the air as these
tender apples simmer.

Peppermint-Coated Pretzels

1 (16-ounce) package pretzel nuggets (we tested with Snyder's of Hanover Sourdough Pretzel Nuggets)
2 (16-ounce) packages vanilla bark coating squares, coarsely chopped
2 cups (12-ounce package) white chocolate morsels
1 (4-ounce) package white chocolate baking bars, broken into pieces
1 (16-ounce) package hard peppermint candies, finely crushed and divided (about 2 cups)
½ teaspoon peppermint extract

● Combine first 4 ingredients in a 4-quart slow cooker.
● Cover and cook on LOW 2 hours. Stir chocolate mixture; add 1¼ cups crushed peppermint candies and peppermint extract, stirring well to coat.
● Drop pretzel mixture by heaping tablespoons onto wax paper. Sprinkle remaining ¾ cup crushed peppermint candies evenly on pieces before they set. Let stand until firm. Makes 4½ pounds or about 80 pieces.

Slow-Cooker Size: 4-quart

Prep: 34 minutes
Cook: 2 hours

Holiday Gift

These pretzels, with their festive candy coating, make great gifts around the holidays. Place the peppermints in a zip-top freezer bag, and crush with a rolling pin. Take your time when crushing the peppermints—you don't want large pieces or fine crumbs.

Bark coating firms up this crunchy candy, and white chocolate boosts the flavor.

Triple Chocolate-Covered Peanut Clusters

1   (16-ounce) jar dry-roasted peanuts
1   (16-ounce) jar unsalted dry-roasted
       peanuts
18 (2-ounce) chocolate bark coating
       squares, cut in half
2   cups (12-ounce package) semisweet
       chocolate morsels
1   (4-ounce) package German chocolate
       baking squares, broken into pieces
1   (9.75-ounce) can salted whole cashews
1   teaspoon vanilla extract

- Combine first 5 ingredients in a 3½- or 4-quart slow cooker.
- Cover and cook on LOW 2 hours or until melted. Stir chocolate mixture. Add cashews and vanilla, stirring well to coat cashews.
- Drop nut mixture by heaping tablespoonfuls onto wax paper. Let stand until firm. Store in an airtight container. Makes 5 pounds or about 60 clusters.

Slow-Cooker Size: 3½- or
4-quart

Prep: 15 minutes
Cook: 2 hours

Freeze It!

Clusters may be frozen up to 1 month.

Get your
chocolate fix here!

Caramel Fondue

2   (14-ounce) packages caramels,
      unwrapped
2   (14-ounce) cans sweetened condensed
      milk
Apple slices
Pound cake squares

● Place caramels in a 3-quart slow cooker; stir in condensed milk.
● Cover and cook on LOW 3½ hours, stirring occasionally, until caramels melt and mixture is smooth. Serve with apple slices and pound cake squares. Makes 4½ cups or 18 servings.

Slow-Cooker Size: 3-quart

Prep: 12 minutes
Cook: 3 hours, 30 minutes

Party Plan

Keep this fondue warm in the slow cooker for easy dipping. Reheat any leftovers in the microwave, stirring at 1-minute intervals until heated through.

Make fondue the
hit of the party at
your next gathering.

White Chocolate-Coconut Fondue

For this supersweet fondue we preferred not-so-sweet dippers, such as fresh pineapple chunks, graham cracker sticks, cubes of buttery pound cake, and dried apricots.

Slow-Cooker Size: 3-quart

Prep: 11 minutes
Cook: 1 hour

Party Tip

For a fun presentation, omit the toasted coconut at the end of the cooking time; have guests dip their treats in the fondue and then roll them in toasted coconut.

1   (14-ounce) can sweetened condensed milk
½   cup coconut milk
2   tablespoons light rum
6   (4-ounce) packages white chocolate baking bars, broken into large pieces
1   (8.8-ounce) container mascarpone cheese, softened
1   cup sweetened flaked coconut, toasted
½   teaspoon coconut extract

• Combine first 3 ingredients in a 3-quart slow cooker. Stir in chocolate and cheese.
• Cover and cook on LOW 1 hour. Stir until melted and smooth. Stir in toasted coconut and coconut extract. Keep warm until ready to serve. Makes 5½ cups or 22 servings.

living light

Eat healthy without sacrificing great flavor with this collection of lightened favorites.

Steamed Brown Bread with Currants and Walnuts

½   cup all-purpose flour
½   cup whole wheat flour
½   cup yellow cornmeal
¾   teaspoon ground cinnamon
½   teaspoon baking soda
½   teaspoon salt
1   cup low-fat buttermilk
⅓   cup molasses
½   cup dried currants
2   tablespoons chopped walnuts
Vegetable cooking spray

● Combine first 6 ingredients in a large bowl, and make a well in center of mixture. Combine buttermilk and molasses; stir well. Add to flour mixture, stirring just until moistened. Fold in currants and walnuts.

● Spoon the mixture into a 2-quart soufflé dish lightly sprayed with cooking spray. Cover dish with aluminum foil. Place a rack and 1 cup hot water in a 6-quart round slow cooker. Place soufflé dish in cooker on rack.

● Cover and cook on HIGH 2 hours and 50 minutes or until a wooden pick inserted in center comes out clean. Remove dish from cooker. Cool, covered, in dish on a wire rack for 5 minutes. Remove bread from dish, and cool completely on wire rack. Makes 8 servings.

Per serving: Calories 175 (9% from fat); Fat 1.8g (sat 0.3g, mono 0.4g, poly 0.9g); Protein 4.4g; Carb 36.8g; Fiber 2.6g; Chol 1mg; Iron 2.0mg; Sodium 263mg; Calc 79mg

Slow-Cooker Size: round 6-quart

Prep: 8 minutes
Cook: 2 hours, 50 minutes
Other: 5 minutes

Test Kitchen Secret

Baking this bread in a soufflé dish in a water bath in your slow cooker helps the bread cook evenly.

Quick Menu

• Bacon
• Orange juice

Flank Steak Wraps with Cranberry-Raspberry Salsa

¼   cup chili sauce
¼   cup lime juice
3   drops of hot pepper sauce
1   (1.25-ounce) package low-sodium taco
     seasoning mix
2   pounds flank steak
¾   cup (2-inch) sliced green onions
½   cup fresh cilantro sprigs
1   tablespoon chopped seeded jalapeño
     pepper
1   tablespoon lime juice
1   teaspoon ground cumin
1   (12-ounce) carton cranberry-orange
     crushed fruit (we tested with Ocean
     Spray)
16 (6-inch) flour tortillas
Garnishes: cilantro sprigs, lime wedges

• Combine first 4 ingredients in a small bowl. Trim fat from steak. Place steak in a 3-quart slow cooker; add chili sauce mixture, turning the steak to coat.
• Cover and cook on HIGH 1 hour. Reduce heat to LOW, and cook 9 hours.
• Meanwhile, combine onions, cilantro, and jalapeño pepper in a food processor, and pulse 5 times or until finely chopped. Add 1 tablespoon lime juice, cumin, and crushed fruit; process until smooth. Spoon mixture into a bowl; cover and chill.
• Remove steak from slow cooker. Slice steak, and return to cooker. Warm tortillas according to package directions. Spread about 1½ tablespoons salsa over each tortilla. Place sliced steak evenly down center of each tortilla; roll up. Garnish with cilantro sprigs and lime wedges, if desired. Makes 16 wraps.

Per wrap: Calories 243 (24% from fat); Fat 6.3g (sat 2.2g, mono 2.8g, poly 0.5g); Protein 14.5g; Carb 30.9g; Fiber 1.3g; Chol 22mg; Iron 1.9mg; Sodium 415mg; Calc 52mg

Red Sauce and Meatballs

1   (25.6-ounce) package frozen meatballs, thawed
1   cup frozen chopped onion
3   (28-ounce) cans crushed tomatoes
1   cup Merlot or other dry red wine
1   tablespoon sugar
1   tablespoon dried parsley flakes
1   teaspoon dried basil
1   teaspoon dried oregano
1   teaspoon bottled minced garlic
½   teaspoon salt
½   teaspoon pepper
2   teaspoons extra-virgin olive oil
14 cups hot cooked spaghetti (28 ounces uncooked spaghetti)
Parmesan cheese

- Combine first 12 ingredients in a 6-quart slow cooker.
- Cover and cook on LOW 4 hours. Serve over hot cooked pasta, and sprinkle with Parmesan cheese. Makes 14 servings (serving size: 1 cup meatball sauce and 1 cup spaghetti).

Per serving: Calories 474 (36% from fat); Fat 18.9g (sat 8.3g, mono 1.1g, poly 0.4g); Protein 21.5g; Carb 56.8g; Fiber 9.1g; Chol 51mg; Iron 5.2mg; Sodium 867mg; Calc 180mg

Pork Roast with Three-Mushroom Ragout

Slow-Cooker Size: 5-quart

Prep: 20 minutes
Cook: 8 hours

Quick Menu
• Roasted asparagus

1	(3½-ounce) package shiitake mushrooms
¼	cup all-purpose flour
1	cup canned crushed tomatoes, divided
2	tablespoons chopped fresh or 2 teaspoons dried thyme
2	(8-ounce) packages button mushrooms, cut in half
1	(8-ounce) package cremini mushrooms, cut in half
1	large onion, cut into 8 wedges
½	ounce dried tomatoes, packed without oil, quartered (about 6)
1¾	pounds boneless pork loin roast
½	teaspoon salt
¼	teaspoon pepper
5	cups hot cooked medium egg noodles (about 4 cups uncooked pasta)

• Discard shiitake mushroom stems; cut caps into quarters. Combine flour, ½ cup crushed tomatoes, and thyme in a 5-quart slow cooker; stir well with a whisk. Add all mushrooms, onion, and dried tomatoes.

• Trim fat from pork. Sprinkle pork with salt and pepper; place on top of mushroom mixture. Pour remaining ½ cup crushed tomatoes over pork.

• Cover and cook on HIGH 1 hour. Reduce heat to LOW, and cook 7 hours. Remove pork from slow cooker; cut into slices. Serve over noodles. Makes 5 servings (serving size: 3 ounces pork, 1 cup sauce, and 1 cup noodles).

Per serving: Calories 503 (36% from fat); Fat 20.2g (sat 6.7g, mono 8.6g, poly 2.5g); Protein 41.2g; Carb 38.0g; Fiber 2.7g; Chol 123mg; Iron 4.2mg; Sodium 406mg; Calc 73mg

Thyme-Scented Pork Chops with Plum Salsa

4   (4-ounce) boneless center-cut pork loin
        chops (½-inch-thick)
¼   teaspoon garlic powder
2   teaspoons chopped fresh thyme
½   teaspoon salt
¼   teaspoon pepper
1   cup low-sodium fat-free chicken broth
¾   cup pitted, chopped plums (2 large)
1   tablespoon fresh lime juice
2   tablespoons chopped tomato
2   tablespoons chopped green onion
        (1 onion)
2   tablespoons light brown sugar
4   drops of hot sauce

● Sprinkle both sides of pork chops with garlic powder and next 3 ingredients. Place chops in a 3½-quart slow cooker; add broth.
● Cover and cook on HIGH 1 hour. Reduce heat to LOW, and cook 2 hours or until chops are tender.
● Meanwhile, toss together plums and remaining 5 ingredients in a bowl. Cover and chill.
● Remove chops from slow cooker. Spoon about ¼ cup salsa over each chop. Serve immediately. Makes 4 servings.

Per serving: Calories 183 (26% from fat); Fat 5.2g (sat 1.8g, mono 2.0g, poly 0.5g); Protein 23.6g; Carb 9.9g; Fiber 0.3g; Chol 59mg; Iron 0.7mg; Sodium 513mg; Calc 23mg

Slow-Cooker Size: 3½-quart

Prep: 12 minutes
Cook: 3 hours

Serving Suggestion
You can also serve this tangy plum salsa over grilled chicken or fish.

Quick Menu
• Couscous
• Spinach salad

Lentils with Garlic and Rosemary

Slow-Cooker Size: 4-quart

Prep: 10 minutes
Cook: 3 hours

Quick Menu
• Sliced tomatoes
• Crusty French bread

5	cups water
3	cups chopped onion
2	cups diced cooked ham
1	cup diced carrot
1	teaspoon fresh or dried rosemary, crushed
¾	teaspoon rubbed sage
¼	teaspoon pepper
1	pound dried lentils
1	(14-ounce) can fat-free beef broth
2	garlic cloves, chopped
1	bay leaf

Garnish: fresh rosemary sprig

● Combine first 11 ingredients in a 4-quart slow cooker.
● Cover and cook on HIGH 3 hours or until lentils are tender. Remove and discard bay leaf. Garnish with rosemary, if desired. Makes 11 servings (serving size: 1 cup).

Per serving: Calories 211 (12% from fat); Fat 2.8g (sat 0.9g, mono 1.2g, poly 0.6g); Protein 17.8g; Carb 30.0g; Fiber 10.5g; Chol 15mg; Iron 4.5mg; Sodium 405mg; Calc 41mg

A little diced
ham adds lots of
flavor to these lentils.

Slow-Roasted Rosemary and Garlic Chicken

10 garlic cloves, minced
2   tablespoons chopped fresh rosemary
1   (5- to 6-pound) roasting chicken
¼   cup orange juice
1   tablespoon balsamic vinegar

- Combine minced garlic and chopped rosemary. Remove and discard giblets and neck from chicken. Rinse chicken with cold water; pat dry. Trim excess fat. Cut chicken in half lengthwise. Starting at neck cavity, loosen skin from breasts and drumsticks by inserting fingers, gently pushing between skin and meat. Rub garlic mixture under loosened skin over breasts and drumsticks. Place chicken halves, breast sides down, in a 4- or 5-quart slow cooker.
- Cover and cook on HIGH 1 hour. Reduce heat to LOW, and cook 7 hours. Remove chicken from slow cooker, reserving drippings. Discard skin from chicken.
- Place a zip-top freezer bag inside a 2-cup glass measuring cup. Pour drippings into bag; let stand 10 minutes (fat will rise to the top). Seal bag; carefully snip off 1 bottom corner of bag. Drain drippings into a small saucepan, stopping before fat layer reaches opening; discard fat. Add orange juice and vinegar to saucepan; bring to a boil. Reduce heat; simmer 10 minutes. Makes 6 servings (serving size: 3 ounces chicken and ⅓ cup sauce).

Per serving: Calories 233 (20% from fat); Fat 5.3g (sat 1.3g, mono 1.6g, poly 1.3g); Protein 39.7g; Carb 4.0g; Fiber 0.3g; Chol 125mg; Iron 2.2mg; Sodium 147mg; Calc 36mg

Slow-Cooker Size: 4- or 5-quart

Prep: 25 minutes
Cook: 8 hours
Other: 10 minutes

Leftover Delight

Chop leftover chicken to use in recipes calling for cooked chicken.

Saucy Chicken over Rice

6   chicken drumsticks (about 1½ pounds), skinned
6   chicken thighs (about 3 pounds), skinned
⅓   cup dry white wine
¼   cup chopped instant onion
2   teaspoons chicken bouillon granules
½   teaspoon dried Italian seasoning
½   teaspoon salt-free lemon-herb seasoning
¼   teaspoon garlic powder
¼   teaspoon dried tarragon
¼   teaspoon dried crushed red pepper
1   (14½-ounce) can stewed tomatoes, undrained and chopped
6   cups hot cooked rice

● Trim fat from chicken. Place chicken in a 4- or 5-quart slow cooker; stir in wine and next 8 ingredients.
● Cover and cook on HIGH 1 hour. Reduce heat to LOW, and cook 3½ hours. Serve chicken and tomato sauce over rice. Makes 6 servings (serving size: 1 chicken drumstick, 1 chicken thigh, about ½ cup sauce, and 1 cup rice).

Per serving: Calories 495 (30% from fat); Fat 16.6g (sat 4.6g, mono 6.1g, poly 3.8g); Protein 50.1g; Carb 32.0g; Fiber 1.6g; Chol 167mg; Iron 4.7mg; Sodium 364mg; Calc 52mg

Sweet Glazed Chicken Thighs

2 tablespoons butter, melted
1 cup pineapple juice
2 tablespoons light brown sugar
2 tablespoons soy sauce
2 pounds skinned and boned chicken
     thighs
¾ teaspoon salt
½ teaspoon pepper
¼ cup water
3 tablespoons cornstarch

- Whisk together first 4 ingredients in a small bowl; set aside.
- Sprinkle chicken thighs evenly with salt and pepper; place in a lightly greased 4-quart slow cooker. Pour pineapple mixture over chicken.
- Cover and cook on HIGH 1 hour. Reduce heat to LOW, and cook 5 hours or until chicken is tender.
- Remove chicken to a serving platter, using a slotted spoon. Whisk together water and cornstarch in a small bowl; add to sauce in slow cooker. Increase heat to HIGH. Whisk constantly until sauce begins to thicken, about 6 minutes. Spoon sauce evenly over chicken. Makes 6 servings.

Per serving: Calories 267 (33% from fat); Fat 9.7g (sat 3.4g, mono 3.4g, poly 1.6g); Protein 30.2g; Carb 12.9g; Fiber 0.2g; Chol 136mg; Iron 1.9mg; Sodium 561mg; Calc 28mg

Slow-Cooker Size: 4-quart

Prep: 10 minutes
Cook: 6 hours, 6 minutes

Quick Menu

- Brown rice
- Wilted spinach

Milwaukee Sausage 'n' Kraut Supper

1½ pounds low-fat turkey kielbasa, cut into 3-inch pieces
3   (10-ounce) cans Bavarian-style sauerkraut, rinsed and drained
3   large Granny Smith apples, cored, peeled, and cut crosswise into rings
1   medium onion, thinly sliced and separated into rings
1   (14-ounce) can fat-free chicken broth
½   teaspoon caraway seeds
8   medium-size red potatoes (about 3½ pounds), peeled and quartered
¾   cup water
Garnish: chopped parsley

• Place half of sausage in a 6-quart slow cooker; top with sauerkraut, remaining sausage, apple slices, and onion rings. Pour broth over mixture, and sprinkle with caraway seeds.
• Cover and cook on HIGH 4 hours or until apples and onion are tender.
• Meanwhile, place potatoes in a large microwave-safe bowl with ¾ cup water. Cover loosely with heavy-duty plastic wrap, and microwave at HIGH 10 minutes. Stir; cover and microwave 5 more minutes. Drain.
• Arrange sausage mixture and potatoes on individual plates. Garnish with parsley, if desired. Makes 8 servings (serving size: 1½ cups sausage mixture and 1 cup potatoes).

Per serving: Calories 271 (16% from fat); Fat 4.7g (sat 2.3g, mono 0g, poly 0g); Protein 15.4g; Carb 46.4g; Fiber 3.9g; Chol 21mg; Iron 1.0mg; Sodium 701mg; Calc 128mg

Slow-Cooker Size: 6-quart

Prep: 20 minutes
Cook: 4 hours

Quick Menu
• Steamed Brown Bread with Currants and Walnuts (page 197)

Set up a **second slow cooker** for the brown bread to accompany this one-dish meal.

Turkey Fajitas

Slow-Cooker Size: 2½-quart

Prep: 15 minutes
Cook: 4 hours

Kids Can Do It!

Let kids show their creativity when these fajitas are ready to serve. Allow them to be in charge of the toppings—fajita decorating!

3 turkey tenderloins (about 2 pounds)
1 (1.25-ounce) package taco seasoning mix
1 celery rib, chopped
1 onion, chopped
1 (14½-ounce) can mild diced tomatoes and green chiles, undrained
1 cup (4 ounces) shredded reduced-fat Cheddar cheese
8 (7½-inch) flour tortillas
Toppings: shredded lettuce, light sour cream, sliced olives, chopped tomato

● Cut turkey into 2½-inch strips. Place in a zip-top plastic bag. Add taco seasoning; seal and shake to coat.
● Place turkey, celery, and onion in a 2½-quart slow cooker. Stir in tomatoes and green chiles.
● Cover and cook on HIGH 4 hours. Stir in cheese.
● Warm tortillas according to package directions. Spoon turkey mixture evenly in center of each tortilla; roll up. Serve with desired toppings. Makes 8 servings.

Per serving (without toppings): Calories 352 (21% from fat); Fat 8.1g (sat 2.9g, mono 1.9g, poly 0.6g); Protein 36.4g; Carb 34.1g; Fiber 2.5g; Chol 55mg; Iron 3.3mg; Sodium 738mg; Calc 178mg

Vegetable-Chickpea Curry

1 (10-ounce) package frozen diced onions
3 carrots, cut into ¼-inch pieces
2 (15½-ounce) cans chickpeas, rinsed and
    drained
1 large baking potato, peeled and diced
    (about 1 pound)
1 cup fresh green beans, cut into 1-inch
    pieces
1 serrano chili pepper, minced
1 teaspoon minced fresh ginger
2 garlic cloves, minced
1 (14.5-ounce) can diced tomatoes with
    green peppers, celery, and onion,
    undrained
1 (14-ounce) can vegetable broth
1 teaspoon salt
¼ teaspoon black pepper
1 tablespoon curry powder
1 cup light coconut milk
3 cups fresh baby spinach

Slow-Cooker Size: 5-quart

Prep: 20 minutes
Cook: 8 hours, 15 minutes

Quick Menu
• Basmati rice or couscous
• Crusty hard roll

• Combine first 13 ingredients in a 5-quart slow cooker.
Cover and cook on LOW 8 hours.
• Stir in coconut milk and spinach.
• Cover and cook on HIGH 15 minutes or until heated.
Makes 8 servings.

Per serving: Calories 170 (17% from fat); Fat 3.4g (sat 1.5g, mono 0.6g, poly 0.9g); Protein 6.2g; Carb 31.1g;
Fiber 5.8g; Chol 0mg; Iron 2.4mg; Sodium 904mg; Calc 82mg

A delicious aroma
    fills your home
  as this slow-cooked
Indian delight simmers.

Barley-Stuffed Cabbage Rolls with Pine Nuts and Currants

Trimming part of the thick center vein from each cabbage leaf makes the leaves more pliable and easier to roll up.

Slow-Cooker Size: 5-quart

Prep: 25 minutes
Cook: 2 hours or 6 hours

Make-Ahead Tip

Assemble the cabbage rolls the night before to get a head start on the next day's dinner. Cover and chill them in an airtight container until ready to cook. (Do not chill them in the slow-cooker crock.)

1   large head fresh green cabbage, cored
1   tablespoon olive oil
1½   cups finely chopped onion
3   cups cooked pearl barley
¾   cup crumbled feta cheese
½   cup dried currants
2   tablespoons pine nuts, toasted
2   tablespoons chopped fresh parsley
½   teaspoon salt, divided
¼   teaspoon pepper, divided
½   cup apple juice
1   tablespoon cider vinegar
1   (14½-ounce) can crushed tomatoes, undrained

● Steam cabbage head 8 minutes; cool slightly. Remove 16 leaves from cabbage head; reserve remaining cabbage for other uses. Cut off raised portion of center vein of each cabbage leaf (do not cut out vein); set trimmed cabbage leaves aside.
● Heat oil in a large nonstick skillet over medium heat. Add onion; cover and cook 6 minutes or until tender. Remove from heat; stir in barley and next 4 ingredients. Stir in ¼ teaspoon salt and ⅛ teaspoon pepper.
● Place cabbage leaves on a flat surface; spoon about ⅓ cup barley mixture into center of each cabbage leaf. Fold in edges of leaves over barley mixture; roll up. Arrange cabbage rolls in a 5-quart slow cooker.
● Combine remaining ¼ teaspoon salt, remaining ⅛ teaspoon pepper, apple juice, vinegar, and tomatoes; pour evenly over cabbage rolls. Cover and cook on HIGH 2 hours or on LOW 6 hours or until thoroughly heated. Makes 4 servings (serving size: 4 cabbage rolls and 2 tablespoons sauce).

Per serving: Calories 478 (26% from fat); Fat 14.0g (sat 5.1g, mono 4.8g, poly 2.6g); Protein 14.8g; Carb 83.3g; Fiber 8.8g; Chol 25mg; Iron 6.2mg; Sodium 805mg; Calc 368mg

Lamb-and-Black Bean Chili

1   pound lean ground lamb
1   cup chopped onion
2   garlic cloves, minced
3   (15-ounce) cans black beans, rinsed and
       drained
2   (14½-ounce) cans diced tomatoes
1   (14-ounce) can low-sodium beef broth
⅓   cup dry red wine
1   tablespoon chili powder
1½ teaspoons ground cumin
1½ teaspoons dried oregano
½   teaspoon salt
⅛   teaspoon ground red pepper
Plain yogurt (optional)
Pita bread rounds, cut into wedges or
       cut in half (optional)
1   cup crumbled feta cheese (optional)

● Brown first 3 ingredients in a large nonstick skillet, stirring until meat crumbles and is no longer pink. Drain. Place browned lamb mixture in a 4-quart slow cooker.
● Process 1 can black beans in a food processor until smooth; add to slow cooker. Stir in remaining black beans, tomatoes, and next 7 ingredients.
● Cover and cook on LOW 8 hours. Serve with yogurt, pita bread, and feta cheese, if desired. Makes 8 servings.

Per serving: Calories 249 (49% from fat); Fat 13.6g (sat 5.8g, mono 5.5g, poly 1.1g); Protein 14.7g; Carb 20.4g; Fiber 6.8g; Chol 41mg; Iron 3.0mg; Sodium 581mg; Calc 71mg

Slow-Cooker Size: 4-quart

Prep: 15 minutes
Cook: 8 hours

Substitution Suggestion

Lamb brings a Mediterranean flair to this chili, but you can use lean ground beef as a substitute.

Chunky Sausage-and-Hominy Chili

1¼ cups bottled salsa
1   cup (1-inch) red bell pepper pieces
1   cup (1-inch) yellow bell pepper pieces
1   tablespoon chili powder
1   (15.5-ounce) can white hominy or whole kernel corn, drained
1   (13-ounce) package chicken sausages with habanero chiles and tequila, cut into ½-inch pieces (we tested with Aidell's)
½   cup water
2   cups hot cooked long-grain rice
¼   cup crushed baked tortilla chips
¼   cup chopped fresh cilantro
¼   cup chopped green onions

- Combine first 7 ingredients in a 3-quart slow cooker.
- Cover and cook on HIGH 1 hour. Reduce heat to LOW, and cook 6 hours. Spoon ½ cup rice into each of 4 bowls; top each serving with 1 cup chili, 1 tablespoon chips, 1 tablespoon cilantro, and 1 tablespoon onions. Makes 4 servings.

Per serving: Calories 388 (35% from fat); Fat 15.3g (sat 4.3g, mono 5.5g, poly 3.9g); Protein 18.7g; Carb 46.5g; Fiber 4.9g; Chol 86mg; Iron 3.5mg; Sodium 563mg; Calc 59mg

Slow-Cooker Size: 3-quart

Prep: 14 minutes
Cook: 7 hours

Sausage Sub

Smoked turkey sausage can be substituted for the chicken sausage.

Top each serving with a **dollop of sour cream** if you'd like to tame the heat of the habanero sausage.

Spicy Black-and-Red Bean Soup

Spicy!

If you want to mellow the flavor of this spicy veggie-packed soup, use regular vegetable juice instead.

1½ cups chopped onion
1¼ cups sliced carrot
2   large garlic cloves, minced
1   (16-ounce) package frozen shoepeg white corn, thawed
1   (16-ounce) can kidney beans, drained
1   (15-ounce) can black beans, drained
2   (10-ounce) cans chili-style diced tomatoes with green chiles (we tested with Rotel Chili Fixins)
1   (14-ounce) can low-sodium beef broth
2   (5.5-ounce) cans spicy-hot vegetable juice (we tested with V-8)
½   teaspoon salt

- Combine all ingredients in a 5- or 6-quart slow cooker.
- Cover and cook on LOW 8 hours. Makes 8 servings (serving size: 1⅓ cups).

Per serving: Calories 149 (4% from fat); Fat 0.7g (sat 0.1g, mono 0.1g, poly 0.3g); Protein 7.1g; Carb 32.4g; Fiber 7.7g; Chol 0mg; Iron 1.1mg; Sodium 755mg; Calc 44mg

Spicy vegetable juice
kicks up the heat in
this colorful bean soup.

Chunky Minestrone

3 (14-ounce) cans low-sodium fat-free chicken broth
2 (14½-ounce) cans no-salt-added diced tomatoes with roasted garlic, undrained
1 (15.5-ounce) can cannellini beans, rinsed and drained
1 (10-ounce) package frozen chopped spinach, thawed
1 cup water
1½ cups frozen chopped onion, thawed
1 medium carrot, chopped
1 medium zucchini, quartered and sliced
2 teaspoons olive oil
1 teaspoon dried Italian seasoning
¼ teaspoon pepper
½ cup uncooked small shell pasta
⅔ cup freshly grated Parmesan cheese

- Combine first 11 ingredients in a 4-quart slow cooker.
- Cover and cook on LOW 5½ hours. Add pasta, and cook on LOW 30 more minutes. Sprinkle each serving with cheese. Makes 5 servings.

Per serving: Calories 284 (27% from fat); Fat 8.4g (sat 3.6g, mono 1.4g, poly 0.6g); Protein 16.4g; Carb 37.4g; Fiber 6.7g; Chol 16mg; Iron 3.6mg; Sodium 602mg; Calc 381mg

Slow-Cooker Size: 4-quart

Prep: 14 minutes
Cook: 6 hours

Test Kitchen Secret

We used frozen chopped onion to make sure the onion is not still crunchy after cooking. If you'd rather use fresh, buzz chopped fresh onion in the microwave at HIGH for a minute or two to precook it a little.

Italian Beef-and-Vegetable Stew

Slow-Cooker Size: 5-quart

Prep: 20 minutes
Cook: 6 hours, 15 minutes

Freeze It!

Keep this one-dish meal on hand—freeze leftovers in serving-size containers.

1   (1-pound) boneless top round steak, cut into ¾-inch pieces
8   ounces small round red potatoes, quartered (about 7 potatoes)
4   cups water
1   (14.5-ounce) can diced tomatoes with basil, garlic, and oregano, undrained
1   (14-ounce) can beef broth
1½ cups frozen chopped onion, thawed
2   carrots, sliced
1   medium zucchini, sliced
1   cup dried great Northern beans
½   cup uncooked pearl barley
3   garlic cloves, minced
1½ teaspoons salt
1½ teaspoons fresh or dried rosemary, crushed
1   teaspoon rubbed sage
½   teaspoon pepper
1   cup fresh baby spinach
½   cup grated Parmesan cheese

● Combine first 15 ingredients in a 5-quart slow cooker.
● Cover and cook on HIGH 6 hours.
● Add spinach; cover and cook on HIGH 15 more minutes or until spinach wilts. Sprinkle each serving with Parmesan cheese. Makes 10 servings.

Per serving: Calories 236 (14% from fat); Fat 3.6g (sat 1.6g, mono 1.1g, poly 0.3g); Protein 18.9g; Carb 32.4g; Fiber 7.4g; Chol 29mg; Iron 3.1mg; Sodium 774mg; Calc 126mg

Chunky Beef Stew

This classic French braised beef, red wine, and vegetable stew is made simple and delicious.

2   teaspoons olive oil
12 garlic cloves, crushed
1   (2-pound) boneless chuck roast, trimmed and cut into 2-inch cubes
1½ teaspoons salt, divided
½   teaspoon freshly ground black pepper, divided
1   cup dry red wine
2   cups coarsely chopped carrots
1½ cups chopped onion
½   cup low-sodium beef broth
1   tablespoon no-salt-added tomato paste
1   teaspoon chopped fresh rosemary
1   teaspoon chopped fresh thyme
⅛   teaspoon ground cloves
1   (14½-ounce) can diced tomatoes, undrained
1   bay leaf

● Heat oil in a Dutch oven over low heat. Add garlic; cook 5 minutes or until garlic is fragrant, stirring occasionally. Remove garlic with a slotted spoon, and set aside. Increase heat to medium-high.
● Add beef to Dutch oven; sprinkle with ½ teaspoon salt and ¼ teaspoon pepper. Cook 5 minutes, browning on all sides. Remove beef from Dutch oven.
● Add wine to Dutch oven; bring to a boil, scraping bottom to loosen browned bits. Add reserved garlic, beef, remaining 1 teaspoon salt, remaining ¼ teaspoon pepper, carrots, and remaining 8 ingredients; bring to a boil.
● Transfer beef mixture to a 4- or 5-quart slow cooker.
● Cover and cook on HIGH 4½ hours. Remove and discard bay leaf. Makes 6 servings.

Per serving: Calories 275 (37% from fat); Fat 11.4g (sat 4.0g, mono 5.3g, poly 0.6g); Protein 28.0g; Carb 14.7g; Fiber 3.3g; Chol 89mg; Iron 3.9mg; Sodium 806mg; Calc 62mg

Thai-Style Pork Stew

2	pounds boneless pork loin, cut into 4 pieces
2	cups (1- x ¼-inch) julienne red bell pepper
¼	cup teriyaki sauce
2	tablespoons rice or white wine vinegar
1	teaspoon dried crushed red pepper
2	garlic cloves, minced
¼	cup creamy peanut butter
6	cups hot cooked basmati rice
½	cup chopped green onions
2	tablespoons chopped dry-roasted peanuts
8	lime wedges

Slow-Cooker Size: 4-quart

Prep: 12 minutes
Cook: 7 hours

Flavor Appeal

Peanut butter melds with classic Asian flavors to lend this one-dish meal a Thai flair.

● Trim fat from pork. Place pork and next 5 ingredients in a 4-quart slow cooker.

● Cover and cook on HIGH 1 hour. Reduce heat to LOW, and cook 6 hours. Remove pork from slow cooker, and coarsely chop. Add peanut butter to liquid in slow cooker; stir well. Stir in pork.

● Combine stew and rice in serving bowls. Top each serving with onions and chopped peanuts; serve with lime wedges. Makes 8 servings (serving size: 1 cup stew, 1 tablespoon green onions, about ½ teaspoon peanuts, and 1 lime wedge).

Per serving: Calories 397 (27% from fat); Fat 12.1g (sat 3.3g, mono 3.5g, poly 0.9g); Protein 30.0g; Carb 41.1g; Fiber 1.5g; Chol 67mg; Iron 2.9mg; Sodium 434mg; Calc 26mg

A spritz of lime over each serving makes a perfect accent.

Ranch-Style Beans

1   (1-pound) package dried pinto beans
3   (14-ounce) cans low-sodium fat-free
      chicken broth
1   medium onion, diced
1   green bell pepper, seeded and diced
1   garlic clove, minced
1   tablespoon chili powder
2   tablespoons Worcestershire sauce
½   teaspoon dry mustard
¼   teaspoon black pepper
1   (10-ounce) can diced tomatoes and
      green chiles

- Place beans in a Dutch oven; add water 2 inches above beans. Bring to a boil. Boil 1 minute; cover, remove from heat, and let stand 1 hour. Drain.
- Place soaked beans in a 5-quart slow cooker; add broth and next 7 ingredients.
- Cover and cook on LOW 12 hours. Stir in tomatoes and green chiles. Makes 7 servings.

Per serving: Calories 259 (9% from fat); Fat 2.6g (sat 0.9g, mono 0.2g, poly 0.4g); Protein 17.1g; Carb 44.2g; Fiber 11.6g; Chol 4mg; Iron 3.8mg; Sodium 289mg; Calc 105mg

---

Slow-Cooker Size: 5-quart

Prep: 10 minutes
Cook: 12 hours
Other: 1 hour

Overnight Soak Option

To soak beans overnight, cover dried beans with 2 inches water; let soak 8 hours. Drain and proceed with recipe.

Quick Menu

- Rotisserie chicken
- Coleslaw

Roasted Sweet Onions

4   medium-size sweet onions
3   tablespoons extra-virgin olive oil
1½ teaspoons salt
2   teaspoons chopped fresh thyme
2   tablespoons balsamic vinegar
¼   teaspoon freshly ground pepper

- Cut each onion into 8 wedges or 6 slices. Place onion in a lightly greased 6-quart oval slow cooker; drizzle with olive oil. Sprinkle evenly with salt and thyme. Drizzle with balsamic vinegar; sprinkle with pepper.
- Cover and cook on HIGH 4 hours or until browned and tender. Serve with steak or pork chops. Makes 6 servings.

Per serving: Calories 107 (59% from fat); Fat 7.0g (sat 1.0g, mono 5.4g, poly 0.6g); Protein 1.4g; Carb 10.2g; Fiber 2.1g; Chol 0mg; Iron 0.3mg; Sodium 586mg; Calc 30mg

Slow-Cooker Size: oval 6-quart

Prep: 8 minutes
Cook: 4 hours

Test Kitchen Secret

You'll need a large slow cooker for maximum surface area, not depth.

These onions are great **served chilled** on a bed of baby lettuces with balsamic vinaigrette and blue cheese.

Overnight Apple Butter

1   cup firmly packed brown sugar
½   cup honey
¼   cup apple cider
1   tablespoon ground cinnamon
¼   teaspoon ground cloves
⅛   teaspoon ground mace
10 medium apples, peeled, cored, and cut
     into large chunks (about 2½ pounds)

● Combine all ingredients in a 5-quart slow cooker.
● Cover and cook on LOW 10 hours or until apples are very tender.
● Place a large fine-mesh sieve over a bowl; spoon one-third of apple mixture into sieve. Press mixture through sieve using the back of a spoon or ladle. Discard pulp. Repeat procedure with remaining apple mixture. Return apple mixture to slow cooker.
● Cook, uncovered, on HIGH 1½ hours or until mixture is thick, stirring occasionally. Spoon into a bowl; cover and chill up to 1 week. Makes 16 servings (serving size: ¼ cup).

Per serving: Calories 126 (1% from fat); Fat 0.1g (sat 0g, mono 0g, poly 0g); Protein 0.3g; Carb 33.2g; Fiber 1.3g; Chol 0mg; Iron 0.4mg; Sodium 6mg; Calc 20mg

Slow-Cooker Size: 5-quart

Prep: 15 minutes
Cook: 11 hours, 30 minutes

Apple Picker

Using a mixture of apple varieties—rather than using just one type—produces apple butter with rich, complex flavors. Good choices include Granny Smith, Esopus Spitzenburg, Jonathan, Northern Spy, Rome, Stayman, Winesap, and York.

Enjoy this apple butter over toast or English muffins, or serve it with pork chops or chicken.

holiday magic

Ring in the season with family classics, such as sweet potato casserole and turkey and dressing.

Hot Cider Punch

1   (64-ounce) bottle apple cider
2   cups orange juice
¾   cup fresh lemon juice
¼   cup honey
10   whole allspice
5   whole cloves
1   (2½-inch) cinnamon stick
1   lemon, sliced

• Combine first 7 ingredients in a 4- or 5-quart slow cooker.
• Cover and cook on HIGH 4 hours or on LOW 8 hours. Pour liquid through a wire-mesh strainer into a large container, discarding spices. Add lemon slices just before serving. Serve warm. Makes 11 cups.

Slow-Cooker Size: 4- or 5-quart

Prep: 8 minutes
Cook: 4 hours or 8 hours

Spice Bag

For easy removal of whole spices, tie them in a cheesecloth bag.

Honey offers a **natural sweetness** to this beverage.

Breakfast Casserole

1 pound ground pork sausage
1 (28-ounce) package frozen country-style hash browns, thawed
2 cups (8 ounces) shredded sharp Cheddar cheese
12 large eggs, lightly beaten
1 cup milk
2 teaspoons salt
1 teaspoon pepper
½ teaspoon dry mustard

- Cook sausage in a medium nonstick skillet until it crumbles and is no longer pink. Drain and pat dry with paper towels.
- Place hash browns in a lightly greased 6-quart slow cooker. Spoon sausage over hash browns; sprinkle with cheese.
- Whisk together eggs and remaining 4 ingredients; pour over cheese.
- Cover and cook on LOW 4 to 4½ hours or until set. Uncover and let stand 15 minutes. Makes 6 to 8 servings.

Slow-Cooker Size: 6-quart

Prep: 8 minutes
Cook: 4 hours, 30 minutes
Other: 15 minutes

Spicy!

To spice things up, try using hot sausage and Monterey Jack cheese with peppers instead of regular sausage and Cheddar cheese.

Grandma Dean's Chicken and Dressing

Many grocery delis offer baked cornbread; just steer away from the sweet variety for this recipe.

1 (2½-pound) rotisserie chicken, skinned, boned, and shredded (about 4 cups)
6 cups coarsely crumbled cornbread
8 (1-ounce) firm white bread slices, torn into pieces
2 (14-ounce) cans chicken broth
2 (10¾-ounce) cans cream of chicken soup
1 medium onion, chopped
3 celery ribs, chopped
4 large eggs, lightly beaten
2 teaspoons ground sage
½ teaspoon pepper
¼ teaspoon salt
½ cup butter, softened

● Combine first 11 ingredients in a large bowl. Transfer mixture to a lightly greased 5-quart round slow cooker. Dot evenly with butter.
● Cover and cook on HIGH 3 to 4 hours or on LOW 7 hours or until set. Stir well before serving. Makes 8 to 10 servings.

Slow-Cooker Size: round 5-quart

Prep: 29 minutes
Cook: 4 hours or 7 hours

Cornbread Prep

We used 2 (6-ounce) packages cornbread mix, prepared according to package directions, to equal 6 cups coarsely crumbled cornbread. Both mixes can be baked at the same time in a 9-inch square pan.

Homemade cornbread works best in this recipe, but you can take a **shortcut** by using cornbread from a mix or the deli.

Green Bean Casserole

This holiday classic is sure to become a convenient family favorite throughout the year with the help of your slow cooker.

2   (14.5-ounce) cans cut green beans, drained
1   (10¾-ounce) can cream of mushroom soup, undiluted
1   (8-ounce) package shredded Cheddar cheese
2   (4.5-ounce) jars sliced mushrooms, drained
1   cup milk
1   tablespoon Worcestershire sauce
¼   teaspoon pepper
1   (6-ounce) can French fried onion rings, divided (we tested with Durkee's)

● Combine first 7 ingredients in a large bowl; stir in half of French fried onion rings. Spoon casserole mixture into a lightly greased 2- or 3-quart slow cooker.
● Cover and cook on LOW 2 hours. Sprinkle remaining onion rings on top of casserole. Cover and cook on LOW 30 more minutes. Makes 8 to 10 servings.

Adding the onion rings toward the end of cooking the casserole keeps them **crunchy**.

Sweet Potato Casserole with Pecan Topping

2	(29-ounce) cans sweet potatoes in syrup, drained and mashed (about 4 cups mashed)
⅓	cup butter, melted
½	cup granulated sugar
3	tablespoons light brown sugar
2	large eggs, lightly beaten
1	teaspoon vanilla extract
½	teaspoon ground cinnamon
¼	teaspoon ground nutmeg
⅓	cup heavy whipping cream
¾	cup chopped pecans
¾	cup firmly packed light brown sugar
¼	cup all-purpose flour
2	tablespoons butter, melted

● Combine first 8 ingredients in a large bowl; beat at medium speed with an electric mixer until smooth. Add whipping cream; stir well. Pour into a lightly greased 3-quart slow cooker.
● Combine pecans and remaining 3 ingredients in a small bowl. Sprinkle over sweet potatoes.
● Cover and cook on HIGH 3 to 4 hours. Makes 8 servings.

Slow-Cooker Size: 3-quart

Prep: 14 minutes
Cook: 4 hours

Alternative to the Oven

This is a great holiday side that cooks on the counter-top while your turkey and dressing fill your oven.

Dual Slow-Cooker Menu

• Roasted turkey
• Cornbread dressing
• Cranberry sauce
• Green Bean Casserole (page 232)

A crunchy pecan topping decks creamy sweet potatoes.

Squash and Cornbread Casserole

1   (10¾-ounce) can cream of mushroom
     soup, undiluted
1   (8-ounce) container sour cream
1½ pounds yellow squash, cut into ½-inch
     slices
1   cup chopped onion
1   cup shredded carrot
1   (11-ounce) can sweet whole kernel corn,
     drained
1½ cups cornbread stuffing mix
¼   cup butter or margarine, melted
2   teaspoons dried sage

● Combine soup and sour cream in a large bowl. Add
vegetables, stirring gently to coat.
● Spoon vegetable mixture into a lightly greased 4-quart
slow cooker.
● Combine stuffing mix and remaining 2 ingredients;
sprinkle over vegetable mixture.
● Cover and cook on LOW 5 hours. Uncover and let stand
10 minutes before serving. Makes 8 servings.

Slow-Cooker Size: 4-quart

Prep: 14 minutes
Cook: 5 hours
Other: 10 minutes

Quick Menu

• Cornish hens
• Roasted asparagus

Carrot and corn
are welcome additions to this Southern favorite.

Jalapeño Creamed Spinach

4 (10-ounce) packages frozen chopped spinach, thawed, drained, and squeezed dry
2 (8-ounce) packages cream cheese, cubed
½ (16-ounce) loaf hot Mexican pasteurized prepared cheese product
1 cup chopped onion
⅓ cup butter, melted
2 tablespoons all-purpose flour
1 tablespoon Worcestershire sauce
1 teaspoon salt
½ teaspoon black pepper
¼ teaspoon garlic powder
⅛ teaspoon ground red pepper

• Stir together all ingredients in a large bowl. Spoon into a lightly greased 5-quart slow cooker.
• Cover and cook on LOW 4 to 5 hours. Makes 8 servings.

Mushroom-Rice Pilaf

¼ cup butter or margarine, melted
1 cup uncooked long-grain converted rice
   (we tested with Uncle Ben's)
1 (10½-ounce) can condensed beef broth
1 (10½-ounce) can beef consommé
1 cup coarsely chopped fresh mushrooms
2 tablespoons sliced green onion (1 onion)
2 tablespoons slivered almonds, toasted

● Combine butter and rice in a lightly greased 3½-quart slow cooker, stirring until rice is coated. Stir in broth, consommé, and mushrooms.

● Cover and cook on LOW 4 to 4½ hours. Add green onion and almonds; fluff with a fork. Makes 4 to 6 servings.

Slow-Cooker Size: 3½-quart

Prep: 6 minutes
Cook: 4 hours, 30 minutes

Rice Tips

Thoroughly coating rice with butter before adding broth helps rice grains retain a pleasing texture. Converted rice works best in this recipe.

Quick Menu

● Roasted chicken
● Green beans

Steeped in beef broth and consommé, white rice takes on a **buttery** new identity.

Extra-Cheesy Macaroni and Cheese

Using Italian and Cheddar cheeses updates this family favorite that is sure to please kids as well as impress adults.

1   (8-ounce) package shredded Italian three-cheese blend
1   (8-ounce) package shredded sharp Cheddar cheese
2   large eggs, lightly beaten
1   (12-ounce) can evaporated milk
1½ cups milk
1   teaspoon salt
¾   teaspoon dry mustard
¼   teaspoon ground red pepper
½   teaspoon black pepper
8   ounces small shell pasta (about 2¼ cups), uncooked

- Combine cheeses in a bowl; set aside.
- Whisk together eggs and next 6 ingredients in a large bowl. Stir in pasta and 3 cups cheese mixture. Pour mixture into a lightly greased 3-quart slow cooker; sprinkle with ¾ cup cheese mixture.
- Cover and cook on LOW 4 hours. Sprinkle servings evenly with remaining cheese mixture. Makes 6 to 8 servings.

Slow-Cooker Size: 3-quart

Prep: 6 minutes
Cook: 4 hours

No Precook

The best part of this simple recipe is that you don't have to precook the pasta!

Spiced Apple Butter

Slow-Cooker Size: 5-quart

Prep: 20 minutes
Cook: 12 hours
Other: 8 hours

Test Kitchen Secret

For an extra-fresh home-made flavor, use fresh apple cider from a local apple orchard or the produce section of your supermarket.

8   large Granny Smith apples, peeled and
        cut into ½-inch cubes (about 10 cups)
½   cup apple cider
½   cup granulated sugar
½   cup firmly packed light brown sugar
2   teaspoons ground cinnamon
½   teaspoon ground cloves
¼   teaspoon ground allspice

• Combine all ingredients in a 5-quart slow cooker.
• Cover and cook on LOW 6 hours. Mash apples. Cover and cook on LOW 6 more hours or until mixture is deep brown and a spreading consistency. Cool. Cover and chill 8 hours. Store in refrigerator up to 3 weeks. Makes 4 cups.

A wonderful aroma fills the air when apple butter simmers on the countertop.

Cranberry-Apple Cobbler

Any Time of Year

You can enjoy this festive cobbler year round by using frozen cranberries when fresh are not available.

5	Granny Smith apples, peeled and sliced (about 3 pounds)
2	cups fresh or frozen cranberries
1	cup firmly packed light brown sugar
1	teaspoon vanilla extract
1	teaspoon ground cinnamon
2	teaspoons cornstarch
¼	cup water
1	vanilla bean, split
1	cup all-purpose flour
¾	teaspoon baking powder
⅛	teaspoon salt
⅓	cup butter, softened
⅓	cup granulated sugar
1	tablespoon milk
1	large egg

Vanilla ice cream

● Combine first 5 ingredients in a lightly greased 5-quart slow cooker.
● Whisk together cornstarch and ¼ cup water until smooth; add to slow cooker, stirring well.
● Cover and cook on HIGH 1½ hours.
● Meanwhile, use a small, sharp knife to scrape seeds from vanilla bean, discarding pod. Combine vanilla seeds and next 3 ingredients; set aside.
● Beat butter at medium speed with an electric mixer until creamy. Gradually add granulated sugar, beating well; add milk and egg, beating until blended. Stir in flour mixture.
● Stir apple mixture. Drop flour mixture, 1 tablespoon at a time, evenly over apple mixture.
● Cover and cook on LOW 2½ hours. Serve warm with ice cream. Makes 6 to 8 servings.

Holiday Gingerbread Pudding

Slow-Cooker Size: 4½-quart

Prep: 21 minutes
Cook: 4 hours
Other: 45 minutes

Dual Slow-Cooker Menu
• Holiday ham
• Brown sugar-glazed carrots
• Jalapeño Creamed Spinach (page 238)

1   (12-ounce) French bread loaf, cut into 1-inch cubes
1½ cups chopped pecans, toasted
1   cup raisins
3   large eggs, lightly beaten
3   cups half-and-half
1   cup firmly packed light brown sugar
¾   cup molasses
¼   cup butter, melted
1   tablespoon vanilla extract
2   teaspoons ground cinnamon
½   teaspoon salt
½   teaspoon ground ginger
½   teaspoon ground nutmeg
Spiced Whipped Cream

• Combine first 3 ingredients in a 4½-quart slow cooker. Whisk together eggs and next 9 ingredients in a medium bowl. Pour over bread mixture, stirring well to coat; cover and let stand 30 minutes. Stir again to coat bread evenly with egg mixture.

• Cover and cook on LOW 4 hours or until set. Let stand 15 minutes before serving. Serve with Spiced Whipped Cream. Makes 8 to 10 servings.

Spiced Whipped Cream

1   cup whipping cream
3   tablespoons brown sugar
1   tablespoon pecan liqueur (optional; we tested with Praline Pecan Liqueur)

• Beat whipping cream, sugar, and, if desired, liqueur at medium speed with an electric mixer until stiff peaks form. Serve with Holiday Gingerbread Pudding. Makes 2 cups.

accompaniments

These veggies, salads, breads, and cookies
anxiously await to round out a meal.

Green Beans with Caramelized Onion

1   pound fresh green beans
2   medium-size sweet onions, halved and thinly sliced
2   tablespoons butter or margarine
2   tablespoons brown sugar
1   to 2 teaspoons balsamic vinegar (optional)

• Cook green beans in boiling water to cover 15 minutes; drain. Chill overnight, if desired.
• Cook onion in a nonstick skillet over medium-high heat 8 to 10 minutes. (Do not stir.) Cook, stirring often, 5 to 10 minutes or until golden brown. Reduce heat to medium; stir in butter and brown sugar. Add green beans; cook 5 minutes or until thoroughly heated. Toss with vinegar, if desired. Makes 4 servings.

Buttery goodness
gets a touch of sweetness from brown sugar.

Buttery Broccoli Medley

1   pound fresh broccoli
1   head fresh cauliflower, broken into
     florets
⅓   cup butter or margarine
1   red bell pepper, chopped
2   garlic cloves, minced
2   tablespoons Dijon mustard
¼   to ½ teaspoon salt
½   teaspoon freshly ground black pepper
3   green onions, chopped

• Cut broccoli into florets; reserve stems for another use.
• Arrange broccoli and cauliflower florets in a steamer basket over boiling water. Cover and steam 10 minutes or until crisp-tender.
• Melt butter in a Dutch oven over medium-high heat; add bell pepper and garlic, and sauté 3 to 5 minutes or until tender. Stir in broccoli, cauliflower, mustard, salt, and pepper; sprinkle with onions. Makes 6 to 8 servings.

Prep: 30 minutes
Cook: 15 minutes

Make-Ahead Tip

Spoon broccoli mixture into a greased 11- x 7-inch baking dish (do not sprinkle with onions); cover and chill. Bake, covered, at 350° for 20 minutes or until heated. Sprinkle with onions before serving.

Quick Menu

• Kelley's Famous Meat Loaf (page 107)
• Mashed potatoes

Scalloped Cabbage

Prep: 10 minutes
Cook: 1 hour

Lighten Up

Use light butter, fat-free milk, light mayonnaise, reduced-fat soup, and reduced-fat cheese.

Quick Menu

• Corned beef
• Apple Crisp (page 177)

2	cups crushed cornflakes cereal
¼	cup butter or margarine, melted
1	(10-ounce) package finely shredded angel hair cabbage
1	large sweet onion, halved and thinly sliced
½	cup milk
½	cup mayonnaise
1	(10¾-ounce) can cream of celery soup, undiluted
1	cup (4 ounces) shredded sharp Cheddar cheese

● Stir together cereal and butter; spoon half of cereal mixture into a lightly greased 11- x 7-inch baking dish. Top with cabbage and onion.

● Stir together milk, mayonnaise, and soup; pour over cabbage. Sprinkle with cheese and remaining cereal mixture.

● Bake, covered, at 350° for 1 hour. Makes 6 to 8 servings.

Braised Red Cabbage and Pears

2   pears, peeled and coarsely chopped
2   tablespoons bacon drippings or
        vegetable oil
2   cups apple juice
½   head red cabbage, chopped
1   teaspoon salt
½   teaspoon ground ginger
½   teaspoon pepper
1   tablespoon butter or margarine

● Cook pears in bacon drippings in a medium skillet over medium heat 3 minutes or until lightly browned. Add apple juice and next 4 ingredients; bring to a boil.
● Cover, reduce heat, and simmer 20 minutes. Stir in butter until melted. Makes 4 servings.

Prep: 15 minutes
Cook: 23 minutes

Quick Menu

• Slow-Roasted Rosemary-and-Garlic Chicken (page 205)
• Steamed carrots

Surprise guests with the **unexpected combination** of cabbage and fruit.

Collards with Apples

Prep: 20 minutes
Cook: 50 minutes

Dual Slow-Cooker Menu

• Spicy Marinated Eye of Round (page 92)
• Hot-and-Spicy Black-Eyed Peas (page 161)

2   pounds fresh collard greens, cut into 1-inch pieces
2   garlic cloves, minced
3   green onions, chopped
1   tablespoon olive oil
1   cooking apple, diced
½   cup dry white wine
1   teaspoon sugar
1   teaspoon Greek seasoning
½   teaspoon salt
¼   teaspoon pepper

• Cook collard greens in boiling water to cover in a Dutch oven 30 minutes; drain.
• Sauté garlic and green onions in hot oil in a Dutch oven over medium-high heat until tender; add collards, apple, and remaining ingredients. Bring to a boil; cover, reduce heat, and simmer, stirring occasionally, 15 minutes or until apple is tender. Makes 6 servings.

Greek seasoning puts a new twist on these Southern greens.

Deep-Fried Okra

1 pound fresh okra or 2 (10-ounce)
    packages frozen sliced okra, thawed
Vegetable oil
1 cup all-purpose flour
1 cup cracker meal or white cornmeal
1½ teaspoons salt, divided
½ teaspoon pepper
1 egg
1 cup buttermilk

- Wash okra; drain. Cut off tips and stem ends; cut okra crosswise into ½-inch slices.
- Pour oil to depth of 2 inches into a Dutch oven; heat to 375°.
- Combine flour, cracker meal, 1 teaspoon salt, and pepper in a shallow dish.
- Combine egg, buttermilk, and remaining ½ teaspoon salt in a dish, mixing well.
- Add one-third of okra to egg mixture; remove okra with a slotted spoon, and place in flour mixture, stirring gently to coat okra.
- Fry okra, in batches, in hot oil in Dutch oven until golden (about 3 minutes). Drain well on paper towels. Serve immediately. Makes 4 servings.

Prep: 15 minutes
Cook: 9 minutes

Dual Slow-Cooker Menu
- Corn Pudding (page 11)
- Roasted Sweet Onions (page 225)
- Cornbread

Okra Creole

3 bacon slices
1 (16-ounce) package frozen sliced okra
1 (14½-ounce) can diced tomatoes
1 cup frozen onion seasoning blend
1 cup frozen whole kernel corn
½ cup water
1 teaspoon Creole seasoning
¼ teaspoon pepper

- Cook bacon in a Dutch oven until crisp; remove bacon, and drain on paper towels, reserving drippings. Crumble bacon, and set aside.
- Cook okra and next 6 ingredients in hot drippings in Dutch oven over medium-high heat, stirring occasionally, 5 minutes. Reduce heat to low, cover, and simmer 15 minutes or until vegetables are tender. Top with crumbled bacon. Makes 4 servings.

Prep: 20 minutes
Cook: 20 minutes

Quick Menu

- Kelley's Famous Meat Loaf (page 107)
- Buttermilk Cornbread (page 277)

This Southern favorite gets a **kick** from Creole seasoning.

Roasted Garlic-Parmesan Mashed Potatoes

Prep: 20 minutes
Cook: 30 minutes

Quick Menu

• Italian Pot Roast
(page 97)
• Green Beans with
Caramelized Onion
(page 248)

2 garlic bulbs
Olive oil (optional)
3 pounds potatoes, peeled and quartered
2 teaspoons salt, divided
¼ cup whipping cream
¼ cup shredded Parmesan cheese
3 tablespoons butter or margarine,
     softened
⅓ cup chopped fresh parsley
½ teaspoon pepper
Garnish: chopped fresh thyme

● Cut off pointed ends of garlic bulbs; place garlic on a piece of aluminum foil, and drizzle with oil, if desired. Fold foil to seal.
● Bake at 425° for 30 minutes; cool to touch. Squeeze pulp from garlic cloves, and set pulp aside. Discard garlic bulb.
● Meanwhile, bring potato, 1 teaspoon salt, and water to cover to a boil in a Dutch oven; boil 20 to 25 minutes or until potato is tender. Drain.
● Mash potato, or press through a ricer. Stir in garlic, remaining 1 teaspoon salt, whipping cream, and next 4 ingredients. Garnish, if desired. Makes 6 servings.

The aroma of roasted garlic **beckons** the whole family to the dinner table.

New Potatoes with Lemon-Butter Sauce

Prep: 20 minutes
Cook: 25 minutes

Quick Menu

• Country Pork and Corn on the Cob (page 120)
• Steamed green beans

3	pounds small new potatoes
½	cup butter or margarine
¼	cup olive oil
3	tablespoons minced fresh chives
2	tablespoons minced fresh parsley
1	tablespoon grated lemon rind
6	tablespoons lemon juice
½	teaspoon salt
½	teaspoon pepper
¼	teaspoon ground nutmeg

• Peel a 1-inch strip around the middle of each potato, leaving peel on each end.
• Cook potatoes in a Dutch oven in boiling water to cover 20 minutes or until tender; drain. Place in a large bowl.
• Bring butter and remaining 8 ingredients to a boil in a saucepan over medium heat. Remove from heat. Drizzle over potatoes, tossing to coat. Makes 8 servings.

The subtle, fresh flavors of chives, parsley, and lemon complement almost any vegetable.

Roasted Root Vegetables

1   (1-pound) bag parsnips
6   large turnips
2   large sweet potatoes
1   large rutabaga
6   large beets
1   teaspoon salt, divided
1   teaspoon pepper, divided
2   tablespoons butter or margarine,
      melted

● Peel first 5 ingredients, and cut into large pieces. Coat 2 aluminum foil-lined baking sheets with cooking spray.
● Arrange parsnip, turnip, sweet potato, and rutabaga on a baking sheet.
● Lightly coat vegetables with cooking spray, and sprinkle with ¾ teaspoon salt and ¾ teaspoon pepper.
● Arrange beets on remaining baking sheet; lightly coat beets with cooking spray, and sprinkle with remaining ¼ teaspoon salt and remaining ¼ teaspoon pepper.
● Bake vegetables at 450°, stirring occasionally, 35 minutes or until tender. (Pans may need to be rearranged after 20 to 25 minutes to ensure even cooking.)
● Toss vegetables with melted butter. Makes 8 servings.

Prep: 15 minutes
Cook: 35 minutes

Cooking Tip

We cooked the beets separately to keep them from turning the other vegetables pink.

Quick Menu

• Honey-glazed ham
• Spinach-Artichoke Casserole (page 165)

High heat caramelizes these earthy vegetables to add color and enhance flavor.

Stackable Grits

½ large Vidalia onion, diced
2 garlic cloves, minced
2 tablespoons olive oil
1 (14-ounce) can chicken broth
1 cup half-and-half
1 cup quick-cooking grits, uncooked
1½ teaspoons salt
½ cup (2 ounces) shredded Cheddar cheese
⅛ teaspoon ground red pepper
⅛ teaspoon ground nutmeg

● Sauté diced onion and minced garlic in hot oil in a 3-quart saucepan over medium-high heat until tender. Add broth and half-and-half; bring to a boil. Gradually stir in grits and salt. Cover, reduce heat, and simmer, stirring occasionally, 10 minutes or until thickened.
● Add cheese, red pepper, and nutmeg; stir until cheese melts. Pour grits into a lightly greased 11- x 7-inch baking dish; cover and chill at least 8 hours.
● Invert grits onto a flat surface; cut into 12 wedges. Spray top and bottom of each wedge with cooking spray; arrange wedges on a baking sheet.
● Broil wedges 6 inches from heat 2 minutes on each side or until golden. Makes 6 servings.

Prep: 10 minutes
Cook: 19 minutes
Other: 8 hours

Make-Ahead Tip

Make this dish the day before, and then slice it and broil it 4 minutes before serving alongside your entrée.

Quick Menu

• Pork Roast with Three-Mushroom Ragout (page 202)
• Steamed broccoli

A Southern standby gets a new look in this **impressive** dish that's mostly made ahead.

Tomato-Pasta Salad

5   large tomatoes, diced
½   cup chopped fresh basil
3   garlic cloves, minced
1   (4½-ounce) can chopped black olives
½   teaspoon salt
½   teaspoon ground black pepper
16 ounces penne, cooked
⅓   cup olive oil
1   tablespoon red bell pepper flakes
1   teaspoon minced fresh mint
8   ounces mozzarella cheese, cubed

- Combine first 6 ingredients in a large bowl; top with penne.
- Combine oil, red bell pepper flakes, and mint in a 1-cup glass measuring cup; microwave at HIGH 1 minute. Pour over pasta; add cheese cubes, and toss gently. Serve immediately, or cover and chill. Makes 6 to 8 servings.

Prep: 10 minutes
Cook: 1 minute

Quick Menu
• Easy Spanish Pork Dip Sandwiches (page 124)
• Raisin-Oatmeal Cookies (page 284)

Juicy, fresh tomatoes **celebrate summer** with basil and mint.

Horseradish Potato Salad

Prep: 15 minutes
Cook: 12 minutes
Other: 1 hour

Dual Slow-Cooker Menu

• Barbecue Beef
Sandwiches (page 93)
• Barbecue Baked Beans
(page 152)

4   large baking potatoes
½   cup mayonnaise
½   cup sour cream
2   tablespoons prepared horseradish
1   tablespoon chopped fresh parsley
½   teaspoon salt
½   teaspoon freshly ground pepper
4   hard-cooked eggs, chopped
3   bacon slices, cooked and crumbled
2   green onions, sliced

• Peel potatoes, and cut into 1-inch cubes. Cook in boiling salted water to cover 12 minutes or until tender. (Do not overcook.) Drain and cool.

• Stir together mayonnaise and next 5 ingredients in a large bowl. Add cubed potato, egg, bacon, and green onions; toss gently. Cover and chill at least 1 hour. Makes 6 servings.

Horseradish contributes **pleasant heat** to your barbecue feast.

Greens and Vinaigrette

1   garlic clove, minced
1   teaspoon sugar
⅛   teaspoon dry mustard
⅛   teaspoon salt
3   to 4 tablespoons lemon juice
¼   cup olive oil
¼   cup vegetable oil
1   (16-ounce) package gourmet salad
      greens

● Process first 5 ingredients in a blender until smooth, stopping to scrape down sides. Turn blender on high, and add oils in a slow, steady stream. Drizzle over greens. Makes 4 to 6 servings.

Prep: 10 minutes

Quick Menu
• Flank Steak Wraps with Cranberry-Raspberry Salsa (page 198)
• Lemonade

Make this **simple salad** a staple for weeknight meals.

Tangy Spinach Salad

6	bacon slices
3	tablespoons lemon juice
2	tablespoons brown sugar
2	tablespoons Dijon mustard
1	(10-ounce) package fresh spinach, torn
1	(8-ounce) package sliced fresh mushrooms

● Cook bacon in a large skillet over medium-high heat until crisp; remove bacon, reserving drippings in skillet. Crumble bacon, and set aside.

● Add lemon juice, brown sugar, and mustard to drippings in skillet; cook over low heat, stirring constantly, 1 minute.

● Toss together spinach, mushrooms, and lemon juice mixture in a serving bowl. Sprinkle with bacon. Makes 4 servings.

Prep: 15 minutes
Cook: 7 minutes

Quick Menu

• Cornish Hens with Orange-Cranberry Sauce (page 28)
• Bakery croissants

Warm, **lemony dressing** lightly wilts spinach for a fancy salad.

15 Minutes or Less to Prep • 5 Ingredients or Less

Cucumber Salad with Roasted Pepper Dressing

Prep: 10 minutes

Quick Menu

• Saucy Barbecue Ribs (page 119)
• Corn on the cob

8   cups gourmet salad greens
2   cucumbers, diced
1   small red onion, sliced
Roasted Pepper Dressing

● Combine salad greens, cucumber, and onion; serve with Roasted Pepper Dressing. Makes 8 servings.

Roasted Pepper Dressing

1   (7-ounce) jar roasted red bell peppers, drained
2   large garlic cloves, halved
1   (8-ounce) container plain nonfat yogurt
1   teaspoon salt

● Pulse all ingredients in a blender 5 to 6 times or until smooth. Makes about 2 cups.

Make a double batch of this **creamy** dressing to use as a vegetable dip.

Broccoli Salad

4   cups chopped fresh broccoli
1   medium-size red onion, chopped
¼   cup chopped fresh dill
2   tablespoons capers, drained *
Dressing
¼   cup chopped pecans, toasted
      (optional) *

• Toss together first 5 ingredients. Cover and chill 30 minutes. Sprinkle with pecans before serving, if desired. Makes about 5 cups.

* Substitute 2 tablespoons chopped green olives for capers, if desired; substitute ¼ cup pine nuts, toasted, for pecans, if desired.

Dressing

⅓   cup balsamic vinegar
¼   cup olive oil
1   garlic clove
½   tablespoon sugar
½   teaspoon salt
¼   teaspoon pepper

• Whisk together all ingredients. Makes ⅔ cup.

Prep: 20 minutes
Other: 30 minutes

Quick Menu
• Easy Chicken Cassoulet (page 131)

Cherry Tomato-Caper Salad

1 tablespoon drained small capers
1 tablespoon balsamic vinegar
2 teaspoons olive oil
¼ teaspoon salt
¼ teaspoon pepper
8 large cherry tomatoes, halved
3 fresh basil leaves, shredded
Bibb lettuce leaves
Garnish: fresh basil leaves

● Stir together first 5 ingredients. Drizzle over tomatoes, tossing to coat. Let stand at least 15 minutes or up to 1 hour. Sprinkle with basil. Serve over lettuce. Garnish, if desired. Makes 2 servings.

Prep: 15 minutes
Other: 15 minutes

Caper Tip

Capers taste very salty, so a few go a long way. Reduce sodium by rinsing capers well and omitting salt called for in the recipe, if you'd like.

Dual Slow-Cooker Menu

• Sweet Glazed Chicken Thighs (page 207)
• Toasted Herb Rice (page 169)

This recipe yields two servings with no leftovers. Since the dish is **pretty enough for company**, double or triple the recipe for guests.

Crunchy Romaine Toss

1   (3-ounce) package ramen noodle
      soup mix
¼   cup unsalted butter, cut into pieces
1   cup chopped walnuts
½   cup extra-virgin olive oil
¼   cup honey
⅓   cup white wine vinegar
¼   teaspoon salt
¼   teaspoon pepper
1   pound fresh broccoli, coarsely chopped
1   head romaine lettuce, torn into pieces
4   green onions, chopped

● Remove flavor packet from soup mix, and reserve for another use. Break noodles into ½-inch pieces.
● Melt butter in a jelly-roll pan in a 350° oven. Add noodles and walnuts; bake, stirring occasionally, 10 minutes or until lightly browned.
● Whisk together olive oil and next 4 ingredients in a large bowl. Add walnut mixture, broccoli, lettuce, and green onions, tossing to coat. Serve immediately. Makes 6 servings.

Prep: 20 minutes
Cook: 12 minutes

Make-Ahead Tip

Assemble this salad quickly by toasting the noodles and walnuts beforehand and storing them in a zip-top bag until ready for use.

Quick Menu

● Beefy Bello Soup
(page 72)

Think of the toasted noodles and walnuts in this dish as upscale croutons.

Black Bean Salad

Serve this hearty fresh salad as a side dish with slow-cooker sandwiches or roasts when you want a change from the usual potato salad and slaw.

Prep: 15 minutes
Cook: 5 minutes
Other: 2 hours

Quick Menu

- Tortilla chips
- Chicken Enchiladas
(page 143)

3 ears fresh corn
3 to 4 tablespoons lime juice
2 tablespoons olive oil
1 tablespoon red wine vinegar
1 teaspoon salt
½ teaspoon freshly ground pepper
2 (15-ounce) cans black beans, rinsed and drained
2 large tomatoes, seeded and chopped
3 jalapeño peppers, seeded and chopped
1 small red onion, chopped
1 avocado, peeled, seeded, and chopped
¼ cup chopped fresh cilantro

● Cook corn in boiling water to cover 5 minutes; drain and cool. Cut corn from cob.
● Whisk together lime juice and next 4 ingredients in a large bowl. Add corn, black beans, and remaining ingredients; toss to coat. Cover and chill 2 hours. Makes 6 to 8 servings.

A salad-lover's dream—vibrant colors, fresh flavors, and healthy ingredients.

Buttermilk Cornbread

⅓   cup butter
2   cups self-rising white cornmeal mix
      (we tested with White Lily Self-Rising
      White Cornmeal Mix)
¾   cup all-purpose flour
1   tablespoon sugar
2¼ cups buttermilk
2   large eggs

- Place butter in a 10-inch cast-iron skillet, and heat in a 425° oven 5 minutes or until melted.
- Combine cornmeal mix, flour, and sugar in a large bowl.
- Stir together buttermilk and eggs. Add to dry ingredients; stir just until moistened. Pour over melted butter in skillet.
- Bake at 425° for 25 to 30 minutes or until golden. Cut into wedges. Makes 6 servings.

Prep: 10 minutes
Cook: 30 minutes

Made-Ahead Tip

You can freeze this cornbread in a zip-top freezer bag up to 1 month. Thaw it in the refrigerator.

Quick Menu

- New Year's Soup (page 32)

You'll get **rave reviews** when you serve this cornbread, with its golden crust and tender crumb.

Whole Wheat Nut Bread

Don't be surprised by the heavy weight of this bread when you remove it from the pan. Even though the batter contains no egg or oil, it still produces a moist and tender loaf.

Prep: 15 minutes
Cook: 1 hour

Quick Menu
• Spicy Cabbage-Beef Soup (page 71)

2	cups whole wheat flour
1	cup all-purpose flour
1	cup chopped pecans, toasted
½	cup sugar
1	teaspoon salt
1	teaspoon baking soda
1½	cups milk
½	cup molasses

• Combine first 5 ingredients in a large bowl; make a well in center of mixture.
• Dissolve baking soda in milk; stir in molasses. Add to flour mixture, stirring just until dry ingredients are moistened. Spoon into a greased and floured 9- x 5-inch loafpan.
• Bake at 325° for 55 to 60 minutes or until a wooden pick inserted in center comes out clean. Remove from pan, and cool on a wire rack. Makes 1 (9-inch) loaf.

This hearty bread
is just as good **toasted**
the next day for breakfast.

Cranberry-Orange Muffins

2   cups self-rising flour
1   cup sweetened dried cranberries
½   cup sugar
1   tablespoon grated orange rind
⅔   cup milk
¼   cup vegetable oil
2   large eggs

● Combine first 4 ingredients in a large bowl; make a well in center of mixture.
● Whisk together milk, oil, and eggs until well blended. Add to flour mixture, stirring just until dry ingredients are moistened. Spoon mixture into lightly greased muffin pans, filling two-thirds full.
● Bake at 400° for 18 to 20 minutes or until golden. Makes 10 muffins.

Prep: 10 minutes
Cook: 20 minutes

Dual Slow-Cooker Menu
• Breakfast Casserole (page 229)
• Mulled Pear Punch (page 194)

Leftover muffins are **great for breakfast** or a snack—but don't count on these lasting very long.

Chocolate Chip Cookies

Prep: 10 minutes
Cook: 10 minutes per batch

Portioning Tip

Get perfect-sized cookies every time with no mess: Use a small ice cream scoop for shaping the dough into 1½-inch balls.

Quick Menu

• Open-Faced Meatball Sandwiches (page 108)
• Milk

1   cup butter or margarine, softened
1   cup granulated sugar
1   cup firmly packed brown sugar
2   large eggs
½   teaspoon vanilla extract
2½ cups uncooked regular oats
2   cups all-purpose flour
1   teaspoon baking powder
1   teaspoon baking soda
½   teaspoon salt
2   cups (12-ounce package) semisweet
      chocolate morsels
3   (1.55-ounce) milk chocolate candy bars,
      coarsely chopped
1½ cups chopped pecans

● Beat butter at medium speed with an electric mixer until fluffy; add sugars, beating well. Add eggs and vanilla, beating until blended.
● Process oats in a blender or food processor until finely ground. Combine oats, flour, and next 3 ingredients. Add to butter mixture, beating well.
● Stir in chocolate morsels, chopped candy bars, and pecans. Shape into 1½-inch balls, and place on ungreased baking sheets.
● Bake at 375° for 8 to 10 minutes or until lightly browned. Remove to wire racks to cool. Makes 7 dozen.

Raisin-Oatmeal Cookies

1   cup butter or margarine, softened
1   cup granulated sugar
1   cup firmly packed brown sugar
2   large eggs
2   cups self-rising flour
2   teaspoons ground cinnamon
3   cups uncooked regular oats
1   cup raisins
1   cup chopped pecans

● Beat first 3 ingredients at medium speed with an electric mixer until fluffy. Add eggs, beating until blended. Gradually add flour and cinnamon, beating at low speed until blended. Stir in oats, raisins, and pecans. Cover and chill dough 8 hours.
● Divide dough into 2 equal portions. Roll each portion into a 12-inch log. Cut each log into 1-inch-thick slices. Place slices on ungreased baking sheets.
● Bake at 400° for 12 minutes or until golden brown. Remove to wire racks to cool. Makes 2 dozen.

Prep: 10 minutes
Cook: 12 minutes per batch
Other: 8 hours

Quick Menu

• Shredded Barbecue Chicken (page 134)
• Baked potatoes
• Corn on the cob

Big, chunky cookies pack a healthy punch with 3 cups of oatmeal.

recipe index

Recipes that appear in regular type are prepared in the slow cooker. *Recipes that appear in italic type are cooked traditionally to accompany slow-cooker entrées as part of a meal.*